D0120512

Telling the Bible

To the Gang at GMBT

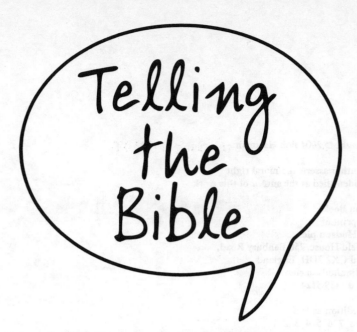

Telling the Bible

Stories and Readings
for Sharing Aloud

Bob Hartman

A LION BOOK

A Lion Book
an imprint of
Lion Hudson plc
Mayfield House, 256 Banbury Road,
Oxford OX2 7DH, England
www.lionhudson.com
ISBN 0 7459 5124 4

First edition 2004
10 9 8 7 6 5 4 3 2 1

Acknowledgments
Scripture quotations taken from the Holy Bible, New International
Version, copyright © 1973, 1978, 1984 International Bible Society.
Used by permission of Zondervan and Hodder & Stoughton
Limited. All rights reserved. The 'NIV' and 'New International
Version' trademarks are registered in the United States Patent and
Trademark Office by International Bible Society. Use of either
trademark requires the permission of International Bible Society.
UK trademark number 1448790.

A catalogue record for this book is available
from the British Library

Typeset in 10.5/14 Aldine721 BT
Printed and bound in Great Britain
by Cox and Wyman Ltd, Reading

Contents

Introduction

A couple of years ago, at a Christian festival, I was asked to read a passage from the Bible before the speaker got up to deliver the evening message. As I sat in my chalet, reading the text, the storyteller in me took over! I saw a line in the passage that made a good chorus – something simple and fun that everyone could repeat. So I reshaped the text with that in mind, and the crowd seemed to really enjoy it.

I was asked to do the same on the following few nights as well, and when I got home, I had a look at some of the other readings and short stories I had written over the years. Many of them were aimed at children or at all-age gatherings, but there were quite a few others that had a lot more to say to adults. So I thought, Why not put them together into some kind of collection? Why not drop in a few suggestions for telling them as well – to make them easier to use? Why not see if others could find some use for them – in worship or in teaching or in small groups or even for personal meditation? And that's where *Telling the Bible* came from.

To be fair, *Telling (a bit of) the Bible* would probably be a more accurate title! There are only about fifty readings and stories here, so the book is not exhaustive by any means. As you will see, this volume is New Testament-heavy, with a particular bias for the works of Luke. That is because those were the passages I was dealing with and that's just how it turned out! What I can say is that I have tried to include readings for the major Christian holidays, and that most of them have been 'road-tested' – usually on the congregation at Bethesda Baptist Church in Trowbridge. In fact, many of these readings arose from my attempts to wrestle with the biblical passages, week by week, in a pastoral context.

As you will see, I deal with lots of different issues in the book. It's quite a personal book, in that sense. You might agree with my opinions on some things, and totally disagree with my opinions on others. So feel free to pick and choose. And also feel free to change, adapt and edit the material for your own particular situation. Because shaping and reshaping lies at the heart of all storytelling.

Finally, some of these readings will still seem more child-friendly than others, and you might feel happier using them primarily in Family Services. I do find, however, that when I tell them to the whole church – and am not specific about which age group they are for – that everyone accepts them just as they are. I also never ask the kids to come the front. If you make the reading for everybody, then everybody will listen! If you'd like more tips on storytelling techniques, you might like to pick up a copy of my book *Anyone Can Tell a Story*.

This is all a bit of an experiment – an experiment I have really enjoyed! But I'm perfectly willing to accept the possibility that some people might not appreciate the kind of playing around with the texts that I have done here. Personally, I find that crawling into a text, asking questions and then coming out the other side, is the best way to discover what it's all about – to be surprised, challenged, moved and won over by what God has to say there. That has certainly been true for me. And as you use this book, as you 'tell' the Bible, I hope that it will be true for you as well.

Death and Regret

(Genesis 3)

**Telling tips: I borrowed this reading from one of my books for
children, *More Bible Baddies*, but I have always used it much more
with adults. When you have read it, I think you'll see why.**

He hacked at the ground with his rough stone axe. He hacked at the
weeds and at the bushes. He hacked till the sweat poured off his
forehead and the calluses rose on his palms. He hacked until he
could hear his heart pounding in his ears. But still the slithering
thing slipped and squirmed away. So he sank down onto a stump
and waited for his breath to return and his heart to stop racing. He
wiped the sweat from his brow and stared at his hands. And that's
when it all came back – the crushing memory of 'before', the pain of
the paradise he'd lost.

It was like a bad bruise. It hurt to touch it, but touching it
reminded him that it was there. Sometimes a smell would trigger it.
Sometimes it would wake him in the night. Today, it was simply the
sight of his hands.

Knuckles gnarled and cracked. Palms rough and swollen. Veins
running down the backs like tree limbs.

Were these the hands, he wondered, that once tended the
Garden? The hands that stroked the lion's mane and traced the
zebra's stripes and danced across the rhino's wrinkled hide as he
gave each one its name? Were these really the hands of Adam?

Sometimes it seemed impossible. Sometimes it seemed too good
to have been true. And sometimes he wondered, How had it

happened? How had he let it all slip between those rough and dirty fingers?

As if to answer the question, a voice called from across the rocky field.

Yes, he had blamed her once. Blamed her more than once. But he knew now that the fault was his, as well as hers.

Eve called again, and then walked slowly towards him. It was almost impossible to see her as she had once been. The years, and the children, and the endless toil it took just to survive had erased for ever the woman who had danced happily in the Garden.

He shut his eyes. He shut them tight. He shoved his fists into the sockets and for a second, just a second, there she was again. Flesh of his flesh. Bone of his bone. Lying beside him on the soft wet grass, at the dawn of their life together. He remembered touching her hair. And her lips. And tracing the shape of her face with his fingertips. And he remembered the prayer he had prayed. 'Thank you, Creator,' he had said, 'for this face and for this morning, and for all the mornings to come.'

'Adam!' the voice called again. 'Adam, why are you sitting there? Get back to work! We have a family to feed!'

Adam winced. There was still a trace of that other Eve in her voice. The same voice that had called out so many years ago – called out across the Garden, 'Adam, come quickly! There is someone I want you to meet!'

That voice was so sweet. The face so innocent and gentle. She skipped towards him, excited like a foal or a fawn. She took his hand (he could feel those fingers, still). And she led him, laughing, to the Knowledge Tree.

There was no reason to be alarmed. No cause for concern. Those words had no meaning then. All was trust and goodness and love. How could he have known? How could either of them have guessed that their new acquaintance would teach them the meaning of those words – and many more awful still.

The Serpent was a handsome creature. Confident. Articulate.

Poised. There was venom in his words, but at the time, his arguments seemed reasonable.

'So the Creator forbids you to eat from the Knowledge Tree?' the Serpent had asked. 'He says that if you do, you will die? Well, what does he have to hide? That's what I want to know. And if he truly loves you, why would he want to keep anything from you? I suspect that he's afraid – afraid that if you eat from the tree, then you will know as much as he does! So why don't you taste the fruit and find out for yourselves?'

Even now, even after all the pain and the toil and the years away from the Garden, there was a part of Adam that still wanted to be convinced. Perhaps the Serpent was right – perhaps the Creator was just jealous of what he knew and did not want to share it. Was it so wrong to want to know? To know evil as well as good?

Adam looked up. His wife was staring at him, and the answer was there, in the lines on her face and in the sadness that never left her eyes. No amount of knowledge could make up for what those eyes had seen: their forced exile from the Garden, the angel with the fiery sword who was there to make sure they could never return, the desolate land they were condemned to till, the murder of one son by another...

Adam looked away and shook his head. His children had often asked him – what did the fruit taste like? Sweet like an apple? Sour like a lemon? How could he have told them the truth? Told them without seeming a fool? That it smelled of decay. That every bite was rotten. That it tasted like death. Death and regret.

Adam pounded his fists against his temples – as he had pounded them a thousand times before.

What if? What if? What if?

What if they had ignored the Serpent? What if they had obeyed the Creator? What if they had never tasted the fruit?

Would he still be wrestling the lion and running with the zebra? Would he still wake up each morning in the soft wet grass and trace his finger across Eve's forever beautiful face?

The thought was simply too much to bear. And so he picked up his axe again and began to hack at the earth. Eve grunted her approval and turned to walk away. But once she was out of sight, he listened again for the hissing one.

The Creator had made a promise – Adam remembered. The handsome one, the confident, articulate creature, would lose his limbs and crawl upon the ground. And one day – surely he was remembering this right – one day, Eve would bear a child who would crush that serpent's head!

But who was this child? And where was this child? All Adam could do was hope. Hope that the Creator's promise would come true. Hope that someone would some day destroy the Serpent. Hope and keep on hacking. Hacking at the ground. Hacking at the bushes. Hacking at the weeds. Because hacking was easier than yearning for what might have been. Because it was better than longing for the life he'd lost when he had to leave the Garden.

I Hear Them Crying

(Exodus 3)

Telling tips: This is the first of a series of Moses stories I did at Spring Harvest's Good Morning Big Top in 2003. I divided the crowd into two groups. One group put their hands to their ears and joined in with me when I said, 'I hear them crying'. The other group joined in when I said, 'I see them suffering' and put their hands above their eyes as if they were watching too. We tried to get louder and louder – or at least more intense – each time we did it. The idea was to put everyone in God's shoes and help them to see the suffering of Israel from his perspective. The contemporary ending is optional, but I found it worked really well in conjunction with the rest of the story. Because situations change, you might want to substitute some other current needs for the ones I have chosen.

At the top of a mountain, behind the mask of a burning bush, God watched the old shepherd creep closer and closer.

He looked an unlikely choice. Unlikely like Abraham. Unlikely like Isaac. Unlikely like Jacob, before him.

But the old shepherd was God's choice. And now it was time to say hello.

'Moses!' God called. 'Don't come any closer. Take off your shoes. For I am the God of your ancestors, Abraham, Isaac and Jacob. And this is a special place.'

Terrified, the old shepherd did as he was told. He slipped off his sandals and covered his eyes. Who wouldn't?

13

And then God spoke again:

'My people are slaves in the land of Egypt.
I hear them crying, I see them suffering.
They work long hours for nothing at all.
I hear them crying, I see them suffering.
Their masters whip them, and beat them, and bruise them.
I hear them crying, I see them suffering.
Their children are taken and murdered in front of them.
I hear them crying, I see them suffering.
I care for my people, I hurt when they do.
I hear them crying, I see them suffering.
And now I have come down to save them.
For I hear them crying, I see them suffering.'

And then God paused. And then God waited. The bush burned dim and low, for God had something else to say. Something sure to send the old shepherd shaking. Something scarier than anything that had happened so far.

'And Moses,' God said at last. 'Moses, you are going to help me.'

(Possible ending)
There was an item in the paper about starving children.
God hears them crying, he sees them suffering.
There was something on the TV about a deadly disease.
God hears them crying, he sees them suffering.
They want to pass a law to kill even more unborn babies.
God hears them crying, he sees them suffering.
The council won't give permission to house refugees.
God hears them crying, he sees them suffering.
And Moses, I know you're an unlikely choice.
And Moses, I know that sometimes you're scared.
But Moses, the bush is burning – like God's passion for
    a world in need.

And the holy place is any place where those needs are met.

So Moses, won't you hear?
Moses, won't you see?
Moses, won't you care?
And Moses, when God comes to save,
Moses, won't you be his helper too?

A Thousand Bricks a Day

(Exodus 5)

Telling tips: Teach the chorus to your group. There is a motion for each line. Two hands to form the shape of a pile. One hand throwing a lump of clay (as on a potter's wheel). And then two hands building up a brick wall. The grunt at the end is, of course, the most important bit of all! Encourage everyone to really go for it.

> *A pile of straw,*
> *a lump of clay,*
> *a thousand bricks a day (grunt).*

The people of God worked hard for their masters. Every day. All day. And if they did not make as many bricks as they were meant to, the slave-drivers would whip them and beat them and bruise them.

> *A pile of straw,*
> *a lump of clay,*
> *a thousand bricks a day (grunt).*

God felt sorry for his people. So he spoke to his helper, Moses.

'I have decided to rescue my people,' he said. 'To lead them out of the land of Egypt. But we must take this one step at a time. Tell Pharaoh, the king of Egypt, that my people must go into the desert to worship me for three days.'

> *A pile of straw,*
> *a lump of clay,*
> *a thousand bricks a day (grunt).*

So Moses did what God said. But when Pharaoh heard, he just laughed. 'The god of your people?' he chuckled. 'Sorry, I don't think we've met. And if I've never heard of such a god, why should I listen to him, or let you leave to worship him?'

'You're lazy, that's all. You and your people! Now get back to work!'

> *A pile of straw,*
> *a lump of clay,*
> *a thousand bricks a day (grunt).*

But later that day, Pharaoh spoke to the slave-drivers.

'Our slaves have asked for a little holiday,' he sneered, 'to worship some god or other. Obviously, they have too much time on their hands. So I think we shall teach them a lesson.

'Up till now, we have given them the straw they need. But from now on, they will have to find their own straw. And they will still have to make the same number of bricks each day!'

> *A pile of straw,*
> *a lump of clay*
> *a thousand bricks a day (grunt).*

So the people of God went to find their own straw. They gathered what little they could from the fields. But with so much gathering to do, there was no way they could make as many bricks.

> *A pile of straw,*
> *a lump of clay,*
> *a thousand bricks a day (grunt).*

And because they failed to meet their goals, the slave-drivers whipped them and beat them and bruised them even more.

'This is not fair!' they cried to Pharaoh.

'This is your fault!' they cried to Moses. 'You told us you came to help. But now you have made things worse!'

A pile of straw,
a lump of clay,
a thousand bricks a day (grunt).

So Moses went to God and told him what the people said.

'I know it looks bad now,' God answered. 'But trust me, Moses, when Pharaoh sees my power, everything will change.

'There is hope. There will be justice. And, one day soon, my people will no longer sing:

A pile of straw,
a lump of clay
a thousand bricks a day (grunt).

But Pharaoh Would Not Listen

(Exodus 7–14)

Telling tips: Because there are so many motions and sounds for this story, I have included the tips in the text. You will need to teach your group the Pharaoh line 'Nyah, nyah, nyah, nyah, nyah!' to start with (and make that really big – like a child who refuses to listen), and warn them about the wave UP and wave DOWN at the end. Otherwise, tell them to follow you through the plagues, and then give them a little time to enjoy each motion when you get there. It might be helpful to have a few assistants in the front with you who have practised the motions, so the rest can follow them.

'Moses,' God said, 'I want you to pass a message on for me. Go to see Pharaoh, the king of all Egypt. Tell him it's time to set my people free. And warn him that if he does not listen, some terrible things will happen.'

So Moses did as he was told. He went to see Pharaoh and passed on God's message.

But Pharaoh would not listen. (*Everyone cover their ears and shout 'Nyah, nyah, nyah, nyah, nyah!'*)

So God filled the rivers of Egypt with blood. (*Make waves with hands – ick!*)

God filled the houses of Egypt with frogs. (*Jump and/or make frog sounds.*)

God filled the skies of Egypt with gnats. (*Make a buzzing sound and wave arms about.*)

But Pharaoh would not listen. (*Everyone cover their ears and shout 'Nyah, nyah, nyah, nyah, nyah!'*)

So God struck the land of Egypt with flies. (*Slap arms and neck.*)

God struck the animals of Egypt and they died. (*Make sad Moo or Baa sound.*)

God struck the people of Egypt with sores. (*Stroke arms.*)

But Pharaoh would not listen. (*Everyone cover their ears and shout 'Nyah, nyah, nyah, nyah, nyah!'*)

So God sent hail to crush the crops of Egypt. (*Make falling/pelting sounds.*)

God sent locusts to eat up whatever was left. (*Make gobbling sounds.*)

God sent darkness to blot out the days of Egypt. (*Look around as if they can't see – hands in front, feeling.*)

But Pharaoh would not listen. (*Everyone cover their ears and shout 'Nyah, nyah, nyah, nyah, nyah!'*)

So God sent an angel to kill the sons of Egypt – the firstborn son in every house. (*Pretend to hold dying child in arms – solemn.*)

And when Pharaoh's son died along with the rest, finally Pharaoh listened. 'Go!' he said to Moses. 'Go and take your people with you.'

But as soon as they had gone, Pharaoh changed his mind.

Still he would not listen. (*Everyone cover their ears and shout 'Nyah, nyah, nyah, nyah, nyah!'*)

He leaped into his chariot and sent his army after them.

Soon the sea stretched out before God's people, and Pharaoh's army rushed, like a wave, behind them. What could they do?

'Raise your special walking stick,' God whispered to Moses.

And Moses listened. Moses listened! He did what God told him, and the sea split in two before him (*Do a wave UP and hold it there*) – leaving a path right down the middle.

God's people hurried to the farther shore, the Egyptian army close behind. And when the last of God's people had reached the shore, God spoke again.

'Lower your stick now, Moses.'

And when Moses did, the waters rushed back again. (*Do the wave DOWN.*)

God's people were free at last. (*Cheer!*)

But the army of Egypt was swept away. Because God had spoken – and Pharaoh would not listen.

I Will Be Your God

(Exodus 16–20)

Telling tips: This reading is all about celebration, so I have tried to make it as much fun as possible. The chorus can be done in a few different ways. The reader can hold out their arms to the crowd, saying, 'I will be your God', and the crowd can respond by holding out their arms and saying, 'We will be your people!' Or the crowd can work in pairs and embrace at the end of each line. Or you can divide your audience into two groups and get one group to represent God and the other to represent the people. It all depends on the nature of the group you're working with, I think. The key thing is to remind them that it is to God himself they are promising themselves here.

I have included suggestions for acting out the different elements of God's provision within the text itself. You could break the crowd up into five groups (to match the first five sections of the text) and teach them each their own little action.

Now that I have set you free, and saved you from your enemies...

> *I will be your God.*
> *We will be your people!*

I'll lead you through the desert to a land of milk and honey. I'll be a cloud by day (*Look up and say, 'Ooh, Puffy!'*), and a fire by night (*Make siren sounds*).

I will be your God.
We will be your people!

I'll feed you when you're hungry, you can count on me. Quail from the sky (*Flap wings and make bird sounds*) and manna from the earth (*You can go 'MMM!'*).

I will be your God.
We will be your people!

I'll lead you to fresh water, you can count on me. Water from a rock (*Make strong pose and grunt*) in the middle of a desert.

I will be your God.
We will be your people!

I'll help you build a tent. I'll give you all the plans. A special place to worship me (*Hold hands in the air*), a special place to meet with me (*Then turn to neighbour and hold upraised hands together to make the shape of a tent*).

I will be your God.
We will be your people!

And I'll give you rules to live by – to treat each other well. No thieving, no killing, no wanting your neighbour's donkey (*Hee-haw!*) or his wife (*Oo-la-la!*).

I will be your God.
We will be your people!

And together we will wait for a prophet just like Moses. Who will welcome (*Reader stretches arms wide in shape of a cross*) all the world to join with our community.

I will be your God.
We will be your people!

And lions (*Everyone roars*) and lambs (*Everyone baas*) will lie down together and the kingdom of heaven will come to earth.

I will be your God.
We will be your people!
I will be your God.
We will be your people!
I will be your God.
We will be your people!

Down and Up

(Exodus 19)

Telling tips: I wrote this originally as a simple Advent meditation, tying together the giving of the Law and the incarnation. You might want to divide the group into two and get one side to do the 'down' motion (two hands above head and down), and the other side to do the 'up' motion (two hands at waist height and then above head).

In the thunder and the lightning,
God came down.
In the shaking and the quaking,
God came down.
Through the fire and the cloud,
God came down.
To the top of the mountain,
God came down.

God came down and Moses went up.
God came down and Moses went up.

In the thunder and the lightning,
Moses went up.
In the shaking and the quaking,
Moses went up.
Through the fire and the cloud,
Moses went up.

To the top of the mountain,
Moses went up.

God came down and Moses went up.
God came down and Moses went up.

Powerful Deliverer – ordinary man.
God came down and Moses went up.

Awesome Creator – humble creature.
God came down and Moses went up.

Babe in a manger – shepherds on a hill.
God came down and Moses went up.

God with us – revealed to us.
God came down and Moses went up.

God came down and Moses went up.
God came down and Moses went up.
God came down and Moses went up.

Under the Thumb

(Judges 6)

Telling tips: Set up a slow, trudging rhythm and get everyone to march along. Then get the crowd to repeat the 'Midian', 'Gideon' and 'Have pity on' lines in the same way as you have said them.

Midian (Midian)
Midian (Midian)

The people of Israel turned their back on the Lord.
They worshipped idols, they ignored his word.
So God let their enemies overcome
and for seven long years they were under the thumb of...

Midian (Midian)
Midian (Midian)

They killed their cattle, donkeys and goats.
They burned up their barley, wheat and oats.
The people of Israel had to hide in caves
but even that couldn't keep them safe from...

Midian (Midian)
Midian (Midian)

Have pity on (Have pity on)
Have pity on (Have pity on)

'Please have pity on us!' cried the people of Israel.
We've done what's wrong. We've gone our own way.
We don't deserve it, but we long for your grace.
Send someone to save us, we pray, from...'

Midian (Midian)
Midian (Midian)

Gideon (Gideon)
Gideon (Gideon)

'Oh, Gideon!' called the angel of the Lord,
'God has something for you to do.
He's chosen you to fight against Midian.
You mighty warrior, he's waiting for you!'

Gideon? (Gideon?)
Gideon? (Gideon?)

'I'm Gideon, yes, but I'm no warrior.
You've made a mistake, you've got the wrong man.
Why do you think I'm hiding in this wine press?
I'm the weakest guy from the weakest clan!'

Gideon! (Gideon!)
Gideon! (Gideon!)

'There's no mistake,' said the angel of the Lord,
'I've written it down on the back of my hand.
"Find Gideon, the guy who's hiding in the wine press.
The perfect choice for God's perfect plan!"'

So Gideon (Gideon)
Fought Midian (Midian)

How's it turn out? That's the question.
We'll just have to wait and see.
But I'll give you a hint – promise not to tell –
It all comes down to God's grace and mercy.

For Gideon (Gideon)
Not Midian. (Midian)
God had pity on (pity on)
His people – just like you and me.

Under the Thumb (Again)

(Judges 6)

Telling tips: Here's another version of the first part of the story of Gideon. It's a little harder to set up than the first version, but it's funnier too! Divide your crowd into five groups and teach each group the lines and actions below. You might want to put the words up on a screen as well. Then simply point to the appropriate group at the correct moment in the text. (And, yes, I know the place is really called Ophrah, not Oprah!)

A. Israelites

We follow God and then we stop;
we're always doing the religion hop.
(Hop.)

B. Midianites

Crush the crops so they can't make bread.
Knock the donkeys on the head!
(Pretend to knock a donkey on the head!)

C. Gideon

I'm Gideon, I'm not your man,
I'm the weakest guy from the smallest clan.
(Look nervous and frightened.)

D. Angel

God will be with you, Gideon.
He'll give you victory over Midian.
(Stretch out angel wings.)

E. Oprah

Today on Oprah, something new,
my mother married a kangaroo!
(Hold up arms like branches.)

Things weren't going well for the people of Israel (A).

They had stopped worshipping God – God, who had brought them out of the land of Egypt – and they were worshipping false gods called Baals instead. So God let them get on with it, and without his help, they fell under the power of their enemy, the Midianites (B).

For seven long years, the Midianites (B) destroyed the crops and killed the animals of the people of Israel (A). It got so bad that the Israelites had to hide in caves. So, in the end, the people of Israel (A) decided to hop back to God again.

'Save us!' they cried. 'We don't deserve it, we know. But send someone to deliver us from the Midianites (B).'

Now, there was a man named Gideon (C) who was the weakest member of the smallest clan in the land. He was no soldier, and no hero either. But God chose him for the job and decided to help him. And that was all that mattered.

Gideon (C) was hiding in a wine press under the tree of Oprah (E). He was threshing wheat there, so the Midianites (B) wouldn't find him. He was scared. He was tired. His feet were turning purple. And that's when he had a visit from the angel of the Lord (D).

God would help Gideon. That was the gist of the message, anyway. The message of the angel (D). Under the tree of Oprah (E). And no one was more surprised than Gideon (C). Under the tree of Oprah (E).

How did it all turn out?

All I can say is that God's grace is amazing. As he showed the people of Israel (A) when he saved them from the Midianites (B) by talking to Gideon (C) through an angel (D). Under the tree of Ophrah (E).

The Fleece on the Floor

(Judges 6)

**Telling tips: Divide your crowd into three groups and teach them
the chorus. Manasseh should have a high, squeaky voice; Asher
a nerd-like voice; and Zebulun and Naphtali (one group for both)
an old man's voice. The idea is that they are not the ideal fighting
force! In the second line, and in the same voice, Manasseh says
'We'll choke you'; Asher says, 'provoke you'; and the Zebulun and
Naphtali group says, 'and try to poke you in the eye!'**

**You also need a volunteer (wearing a fleece!) to play the fleece.
This person sits on a chair, and several other volunteers sit on the
floor. They are the ground. Give one of them a squirty bottle (or
water pistol) filled with water (be careful whom you choose here!).
That person squirts the fleece at the appropriate time in the story.
Don't tell them at the start that the roles will soon be reversed. If
they don't know the story, just let them be surprised! Give the
squirty bottle to the 'fleece' person after Gideon begs for a second
test – and let the revenge begin!**

The Midianites and their allies crossed the River Jordan and
camped in the Valley of Jezreel. It looked as if they were about to
take over for good.

So Gideon blew his trumpet and gathered soldiers from four of
the tribes of Israel.

We're Manasseh / Asher / Zebulun and Naphtali
We'll choke you / provoke you / and try to poke you in the eye!

Now Gideon was no warrior, but even he could see that this was not a promising start. So he asked the Lord for some help.

'Lord,' he prayed, 'you said you would use me to save your people. But look what I have to work with!'

We're Manasseh / Asher / Zebulun and Naphtali
We'll choke you / provoke you / and try to poke you in the eye!

'If you really mean what you've said, if you're really going to help, could you possibly, maybe, give me a sign? Here's what I had in mind. I'll take a fleece, an ordinary fleece, and lay it on the threshing floor. And if, tomorrow morning, the fleece is wet but the ground around it is dry, then I'll know for sure that I can count on you.'

So Gideon laid the fleece on the floor (*Fleece person sits down*). And, sure enough, when he returned the next morning, the fleece was wet (*Shoot fleece with water bottle/pistol*), but the ground around it was dry!

Gideon felt much better. And then he had another look at his army.

We're Manasseh / Asher / Zebulun and Naphtali
We'll choke you / provoke you / and try to poke you in the eye!

So Gideon went back to the Lord.

'Lord,' he prayed, 'please don't be angry, but is there any chance that I could have just one more sign? How about this? I'll put the fleece on the ground again, and this time, could you keep the fleece dry and wet the ground around it? (*Pass over your tissues/towels, everyone!*)

So Gideon put the fleece on the ground, and sure enough, the next morning, the fleece was dry, but the ground around it was soaking wet. (*Fleece person sprays everyone else!*)

'Thank you, Lord,' prayed Gideon. 'Now I know that you will be with us, no matter how impossible this seems.'

And so Gideon, and his army...

We're Manasseh / Asher / Zebulun and Naphtali
We'll choke you / provoke you / and try to poke you in the eye!

... went off to face the Midianites.

Too Many Soldiers!

(*Judges* 7)

Telling tips: Divide the crowd into three groups and get them all to stand. Make one group the frightened soldiers and tell them to scream as loudly as they can at the appropriate part of the story. Then get them to sit down. Make another group the soldiers who kneel to drink. Get them to shake their heads and make slurping sounds. Then get them to sit down at the appropriate point in the story. Make the last group (the smallest perhaps?) slurp water from their hands and then go 'Woof!' They remain standing for the duration.

You can then either let them do the jar (smashing sound), trumpet (trumpet sound), and torch ('Shine, torches, shine' to the tune of 'Shine, Jesus, shine!') sounds on their own, or let everyone join in the fun at the end.

So Gideon and his army set off to fight the Midianites.

'Right then, Lord,' said Gideon. 'We're ready. Well, as ready as we'll ever be.'

But God said, 'Hang on, Gideon. We've got a problem here. You have too many soldiers to fight the Midianites.'

'Too many?' cried Gideon. 'Too MANY?'

'That's right,' said the Lord. 'Too many. I don't want you becoming big-headed over this, you see. Passing out medals and handing out citations and bragging to me about how you beat the Midianites with your own strength. So here's what I want you to do. Tell anyone who's frightened that he is free to go home.'

So Gideon did what the Lord told him. And 22,000 frightened men (*scream AAAH!*) went home.

'All right then, Lord,' sighed Gideon. 'There are 10,000 soldiers left. Ten thousand brave men. Now we're ready to face the Midianites.'

'Hang on a minute,' said the Lord. 'There are still too many men.'

'Too many?' cried Gideon. 'TOO MANY!!'

'That's what I said,' said the Lord. 'Too many. We wouldn't want you getting too big for your britches now, would we? Putting on parades and building monuments because you thought you were big and strong and powerful. So here's what I want you to do. Take your army down to the river. Those who scoop up the water and lap it like dogs from their hands can stay. And those who kneel down and drink straight from the river will have to go.'

So Gideon did what the Lord told him. Some of the men lapped the water like dogs from their hands. (*Slurp and woof!*) But most of them kneeled down and stuck their heads in the river. (*Shake heads and slurp.*) And when it was all over, there were only three hundred soldiers left!

'All right, Lord,' trembled Gideon. 'I guess we're ready to fight the Midianites now. I'll just tell everybody to get their swords, and we'll be on our way.'

'Swords?' said the Lord. 'Who said anything about swords? Look, you can carry them on your belts if you want to, but that's not how you'll win this battle. You see, when this is over, I don't want you going on and on about how fierce you were, how noble and mighty and proud, and about how you don't need me any more. I've heard it all before. If you want to win this battle you'll have to do it my way. So I want you to give each man a trumpet, an empty jar and a torch. Got it? And we'll wait till night, when your enemy is asleep.'

'All right, Lord,' sighed Gideon. But he was less convinced than ever.

'Look', said the Lord. 'If you're still worried, sneak down to the Midianite camp. Listen to what they're saying. And I promise you'll like what you hear.'

So Gideon and his servant Purah sneaked down to the Midianite camp. There were thousands of Midianites, as thick as locusts, more numerous than the grains of sand on the shore. It was not a good start. But when Gideon put his ear to one of the tents, everything changed.

'I just had a dream,' trembled one of the Midianite soldiers. 'I dreamed that a huge loaf of barley bread came tumbling into our camp and struck our tent with such force that it collapsed around us!'

'Barley bread,' said the soldier's mate. 'Surely that bread is the sword of Gideon, and God will give him victory over our whole camp!'

'Yes!' said Gideon. (Well, rather more quietly than that!) Then he and Purah sneaked back to the army of Israel.

'God will give us the victory!' said Gideon to his men. 'I know that for sure now.' And he gave each soldier a trumpet and a jar with a torch inside.

'We'll break into three groups,' he explained. 'We'll creep down around the edge of the Midianite camp. When you hear my group blow our trumpets, then you blow your trumpets too. Smash your clay jars as well and let your torches shine!'

And that's exactly what they did. While the Midianite army slept, Gideon and his men crept down to the camp, and at Gideon's signal, they blew their trumpets (*blow trumpets*), smashed their jars (*crashing sound*) and let their torches shine (*sing 'Shine, torches, shine!'*). Then they shouted together, 'A sword for the Lord and for Gideon!' (*Do so.*)

The Midianite army woke up at once. They were sleepy and frightened. They had no idea what was happening. And in the midst of their confusion, they started attacking one another. They choked each other and provoked each other and poked each other in the eye! And all Gideon's men had to do was chase them away.

And that is how just a few hundred men defeated many thousands.

With trumpets (*blow trumpets*), and jars (*crashing sound*), and torches (*sing 'Shine, torches, shine!'*).

And the help of the Lord, of course!

Oh, Poo!

(Judges 8)

Telling tips: Divide the crowd into four groups (Ephraim, Succoth, Peniel and Israel) and teach each group their little couplet.

Gideon beat the Midianites, the enemies of his people, and it would be nice to think that he then lived happily ever after. But the Bible is not a fairy tale. And so, sadly, he didn't. In fact, he ran into trouble almost immediately.

Gideon's soldiers were hunting down what was left of the Midianite army, when they ran into a bunch of moaners from the tribe of Ephraim.

> *We're from Ephraim, we think you're poo!*
> *We wanted to fight the battle too!*

They felt left out because Gideon hadn't asked them to join his army, and they made a huge fuss, so he let them capture a couple of Midianite leaders called Oreb and Zeeb. Then he buttered them up with all kinds of compliments about how great their grapes were. It seemed to do the trick. But then he ran into the tribe of Succoth.

> *We're from Succoth, we think you're poo!*
> *We're still afraid, so we won't help you!*

All Gideon wanted was a little bread for his men. But the people of Succoth knew that he hadn't yet captured the Midianite kings,

Zebah and Zalmunna. And they were afraid to help until those kings were well and truly out of the way. So Gideon moved on to the next tribe. But he got the same answer from the people of Peniel.

We're from Peniel, we won't help you!
The people of Succoth say you're poo!

This was ridiculous! Gideon had trusted God, he'd risked his life and he'd beaten the Midianites. But instead of being the conquering hero, everyone was criticizing him. And he was getting no help at all! So he went and found Zebah and Zalmunna himself and finally finished off those Midianite kings. Then he went back and punished the towns who wouldn't help him. And at last he sat down to rest.

His troubles, however, were still not over. For there soon came an offer from the people of Israel.

We're Israel, please be our king!
You're quite the opposite of a poo-ey thing!

Gideon sighed. Either the people didn't like him at all. Or they liked him far too much.

'No!' he explained. 'I won't be your king. And my son won't either. God is our king and he alone should rule over us.'

And then, sadly, Gideon stepped right in it!

'I'll tell you what, though,' he said. 'I wouldn't mind a bit of gold. How about you each give me an earring that you took from the Midianites when we defeated them?'

So that's what the people did. And because all the Midianites had worn earrings, they managed to collect quite a pile of gold. Twenty kilos at least! And what did Gideon do with it? He melted it down and turned it into an idol, which was, of course, worshipped by all the people!

Imagine that – after everything God had done! Even Gideon forgot him when things got tough.

As I said, it's not quite one of those happily-ever-after endings. But it doesn't have to be that way for us. Life's hard sometimes – sure. But God is still there – just as he was there for Gideon, if he had only kept on looking. Or to put it another way:

Hang on to God, he's there for you,
Even when life's completely poo!

Good Idea. God Idea

(2 Samuel 7)

Telling tips: There's no participation in this one (not that I can think of, anyway). Just make sure you emphasize those 'O's when you read it!

'O Nathan!' said King David to the prophet one day. 'I've got a good idea! I live in this very nice palace, with cedar walls and cedar sofas and every cedar mod con. But the Lord God has to make do with that tiny little tent we call a tabernacle. Why don't we build him a house?'

'Oh, what a good idea!' said the prophet Nathan to King David. 'You live in this very nice palace, with cedar floors and cedar panelling and that lovely cedar cooker. But the Lord God has to make do with that tatty little tent. Why don't you build him a house?'

But that night, the Lord God spoke to the prophet Nathan.

'O Nathan,' he said. 'I hear that the king has a good idea. He wants to build me a house. I don't mean to sound ungrateful, but I have just one question: When did I say I wanted a house?

'Compared to the king's cedar palace, my tent is indeed tiny, and getting a little tatty too. But it has served me well for many years, and it let me move with my people – from the wilderness to this lovely promised land.'

'Oh,' said Nathan. 'Then what shall I tell the king?'

'Oh – I know,' said the Lord God. 'Tell him I have a better idea. Tell him that I don't need a house, but that I would like to build him one instead! Not a house of stone or brick or cedar, but a house of people. A family that will stretch through all generations. A kingdom that will never end!'

So God built David a house – a family to last the generations. Some of them lived in palaces. Some of them lived in tents. And one of them – David's great great great great great great great great grandson – was even born in a stable!

David's palace is dust. And so is the temple his son Solomon built. But the kingdom that God made goes on for ever and ever.

Good idea – God idea.

They look almost the same. But, OH, what a difference that one little letter can make!

Some Things I Just Don't Understand

Jeremiah 1:5

Telling tips: This is one for two readers: one should say the Bible verse each time and the other can read the rest.

> **Before I formed you in the womb I knew you,**
> **before you were born I set you apart.**

Here are some things I don't understand. I just don't understand.

If, among other reasons, capital punishment is immoral because there is the possibility that an innocent person might die, why is abortion acceptable? Are not all babies innocent? And even if there is just the possibility that what is growing in the womb is a person (just like the possibility that the convicted murderer is innocent), is not that possibility enough to keep us from ending the child's life?

> **Before I formed you in the womb I knew you,**
> **before you were born I set you apart.**

If a person thinks that abortion is acceptable, what do they do when someone they know has a miscarriage? If what is in the womb is not a person – if it is just a mass of cells – how can they honestly express any grief? Is it a person who has died, or isn't it? Surely the unborn child has to be one or the other. Or is it only a person if we want it to be?

**Before I formed you in the womb I knew you,
before you were born I set you apart.**

And why do we always say that a woman has a right to choose what she does with her body? How is the child growing inside her the same as her body? If you take a cell from the woman and a cell from the unborn child and compare the DNA, they will not be identical. The child may be 'in' the woman's body, but on the basis of the best scientific evidence, it's most definitely not the same.

**Before I formed you in the womb I knew you,
before you were born I set you apart.**

And why do we always say that abortion is about a woman's right to choose? Men often use the availability of abortion to force women to part with babies they would rather keep. When your boyfriend or your father or your husband says, 'Get rid of it or you're out!' that doesn't sound like much of a choice to me.

**Before I formed you in the womb I knew you,
before you were born I set you apart.**

And why do we spend thousands of pounds in one part of a hospital to preserve the lives of children born prematurely at 23 or 24 weeks, and then spend thousands in other parts of the same hospital bringing the lives of children of the same age to an end?

**Before I formed you in the womb I knew you,
before you were born I set you apart.**

And why does the phrase 'quality of life' always come up in this discussion? The world is full of people whose 'quality of life' is inferior to ours – people who suffer enormous hardship. But we don't advocate ending their lives for that reason. I have often wondered whether it is really the unborn child's 'quality of life' we are so concerned about – or our own.

> **Before I formed you in the womb I knew you,**
> **before you were born I set you apart.**

Maybe Jeremiah didn't really mean what he said. Maybe he didn't really think that God had plans for him, even while he was developing in his mother's womb. Maybe those words are just poetry.

Or maybe we're the ones who take the poetic licence.

'How's your baby?'

'When's the baby due?'

'Have you felt the baby kick yet?'

We know what we mean. Our language betrays us.

And that's why I don't understand. I just don't understand.

The Boys Who Liked to Say NO!

(Daniel 1)

Telling tips: NO is the operative word in this story. So NO is at the heart of the participation device as well. Tell your group that they are to say NO every time it comes up in the story. Tell them to get louder and more determined each time. Tell them you'd like a really full-blooded rebellion here. And then have a great time!

When the boys lived in Jerusalem, their Hebrew friends knew them as Daniel, Hananiah, Mishael and Azariah.

When Jerusalem was conquered and they were taken as captives to the palace of King Nebuchadnezzar, they were given Babylonian names. And everyone knew them as Belteshazzar, Shadrach, Meshach and Abednego.

But anyone who knew them well, simply knew them as the Boys Who Liked to Say NO!

They were handsome, these boys. And clever and strong, to boot. Sons of Jerusalem's most important families. So Nebuchadnezzar decided to treat them well. He gave them soft beds to sleep on, rich food to eat and an education at his very best university – all in the hope that they would forget about Jerusalem and learn to call Babylon home. And that the rest of their captured people would too.

But Nebuchadnezzar hadn't reckoned on them being the Boys Who Liked to Say NO!

One of King Nebuchadnezzar's servants was an enormous man named Ashpenaz. He had a big belly and a bald head, and more than anything else in the world, he liked to eat! So he was put in charge of turning the Boys Who Liked to Say NO! into good Babylonians.

'For dinner tonight,' he announced, 'you will have the following choices from the king's own menu:

Pink pork sausages;

Plump pork chops;

Or my own personal favourite – Mrs Puffy's Perfect Pork Pies!'

Ashpenaz wiped the corners of his mouth with the back of his chubby hand. The thought of all that food made him quiver with joy. But the Boys Who Liked to Say NO! were calm. They knew exactly what to do.

The king's food looked good, and smelled even better, but they knew it was made from something their Law said they could not eat. The Law they had learned in Jerusalem. The Law their God had given them. The Law and the city and the God they were determined never to forget.

So they turned to Ashpenaz and together they said, 'NO!'

Ashpenaz could not believe it.

'No pink pork sausages?' he asked.

'NO!' said Shadrach. 'But I wouldn't mind a few carrots.'

'No plump pork chops?'

'NO!' said Meshach. 'I'll just have a green salad.'

'And not even one of Mrs Puffy's Pork Pies?'

'NO!' said Abednego. 'But a roast potato would be lovely.'

Ashpenaz wiped the sweat from his forehead.

'The king will be very angry,' he explained. 'If you do not eat this food, you will grow tired and ill. And then there is no telling what the king will do to me. He may throw me in prison, or torture me, or perhaps even take away my daily ration of bacon butties. Please, won't you reconsider?'

'NO!' said Belteshazzar. 'But we promise you that you will not get into trouble. For we will not grow tired and ill. Tell the king to put us to the test. For ten days, the four of us will have nothing but vegetables and water. The other boys in the palace can eat your food. At the end of that time, we shall see who looks more fit.'

Ashpenaz agreed, and so did the king, so for ten days, the Boys Who Liked to Say NO! said NO! to everything but vegetables and water – while the other boys ate their fill of pork sausages and pork chops and pork pies.

What happened? The God that Belteshazzar, Shadrach, Meshach and Abednego would not forget did not forget them either! At the end of the test, the Boys Who Liked to Say NO! looked healthy and strong. And the other boys? Well, their bellies were bloated, their breath was bad, and I can't begin to tell you how they reacted when they discovered what was IN Mrs Puffy's Pork Pies!

So from then on, Belteshazzar, Shadrach, Meshach and Abednego were allowed to eat whatever they liked. All because they were loyal to their God. And because they were the Boys Who Liked to Say NO!

A Mouthful

(Daniel 6)

Telling tips: This reading is just a bit of fun really. But, depending on the age of your audience, you might want to have a short vocabulary lesson at the start!

Cupidity. Cupidity.
This is a tale of cupidity.
The king's advisers were jealous of Daniel.
They wanted that 'power' thing.
So they dreamed up a trick to put Daniel to death
And went to see the king.

Stupidity. Stupidity.
This is a tale of stupidity.
'You're like a god, King Darius!' they said.
You give us all we need!
So why should we pray to anyone but you?'
Flattered, the king agreed.

Royalty. Royalty.
This is a tale of royalty.
'Then what should we do?' asked the puzzled king.
'A new law!' his advisers grinned.
'If we catch someone praying to another god,
He'll be tossed in the lions' den!'

Loyalty. Loyalty.
This is a tale of loyalty.
Daniel was loyal to his friend King Darius.
But he was loyal to God even more.
So he knelt at the window and prayed his prayers.
In spite of the brand new law.

Ferocity. Ferocity.
This is a tale of ferocity.
The advisers cheered when they caught Daniel praying.
They roared with laughter and glee!
Then they tossed him into a den full of lions,
Who were waiting for their tea!

Velocity. Velocity.
This is a tale of velocity.
God sent an angel just as quick as he could
To shut the lions' jaws.
While Daniel slept soundly through the night
Safe from their teeth and claws.

Bonhomie. Bonhomie.
This is a tale of bonhomie.
King Darius was sorry he'd passed the law.
For Daniel was his friend.
So when he saw that Daniel was safe,
He had him pulled out of the den.

Gastronomy. Gastronomy.
This is a tale of gastronomy.
He arrested the men who'd made the law.
He tossed *them* into the den instead.
Then the lions snapped and snarled and roared
And had their breakfast in bed!

Cupidity – Stupidity.
Royalty – Loyalty.
Ferocity – Velocity.
Bonhomie – Gastronomy
(It's a mouthful, I know.)
But that is the story of Daniel!

The 'N' Word

(The book of Jonah)

Telling tips: It's important to say the word 'Ninevites' with as much
disgust or hatred as you can muster. To further make the point, you
might want to get the audience to repeat it after you, as in 'Ninevites,'
he grunted (Ninevites), and so on in the second line of each verse.

Jonah didn't mind using the 'n' word.
'Ninevites!' he grunted, the word like a curse on his lips.
'Why would God want to save Ninevites?
They're cruel. They're brutal. They're hardly human.
And I will not play a part in their rescue.'

Jonah didn't mind using the 'n' word.
'Ninevites!' he grumbled, as he boarded a boat for Tarshish.
'Conquerors. Oppressors. Monsters, not men.
I will not go. That's all there is to it.
They will not profit from this prophet's words!'

Jonah didn't mind using the 'n' word.
'Ninevites,' he whispered, as he eyed each sailor up and down.
'Dull, base and beast-like.
Some of these sailors have that look.
I'd better watch my back.'

Jonah didn't mind using the 'n' word.
'Ninevites!' he explained, as a storm swallowed up the ship.

'I won't take God's message to Ninevites.
That's why we're in this mess.
Throw me into the water and your troubles will be over.'

Jonah didn't mind using the 'n' word.
'Ninevites!' he cursed, as he sank like a stone in the sea.
'Uncaring, unfeeling,
Without an ounce of compassion.
I knew that they'd be the death of me.'

Jonah didn't mind using the 'n' word.
'Ninevites,' he sighed, as he sat in the belly of the fish.
'All right then. I'll go and talk to Ninevites.
I don't like them. I don't want to.
But I guess I've been saved for a reason.'

Jonah didn't mind using the 'n' word.
'Ninevites,' he muttered, as he walked around their city.
'They look funny. They smell funny. They talk funny.
But I'll do what I have to.
I'll do what I promised.'

Jonah didn't mind using the 'n' word.
'Ninevites!' he cried, forcing the word out as cheerfully as he could.
'You have forty days to change your ways.
Or God will destroy your city.'
And the Ninevites repented as one!

Jonah didn't mind using the 'n' word.
'Ninevites,' he sneered, as he climbed a hill outside the city.
'They're faking it. They haven't really changed.
And when they go back to their old ways,
I'll see them destroyed after all!'

Jonah didn't mind using the 'n' word.
'Ninevites!' he grinned, as he sat in the shade of a little tree.
'C'mon, Ninevites. I'm waiting to see you fall.
Waiting to see God's vengeance!'
But in the night, God sent a worm to kill the little tree.

Jonah didn't mind using the 'n' word.
'Ninevites!' he swore, as he looked at his little tree.
'They're responsible for this, I'm sure!
They're wicked and vile. They care for nothing!'
And that's when he heard God's voice.

God had a problem with the 'n' word.
But the 'j' word was driving him mad.
'Jonah,' God sighed. 'Jonah, don't be angry.
The people in that city are people just like you.
120,000 – men, women and children.
If the death of a tree is important
Should I not be concerned about their fate too?'

And that's where the story ends.
Not with an answer, but a question.
Will we love whomever God loves,
Whether we like them or not?

Jonah didn't mind using the 'n' word.
Do you?

Lights and Bells

(Matthew 1-2, Luke 1-2)

**This is just a little Christmas poem for you to tell on your own.
If you want to get the crowd involved, you might let them do
the second line of each verse: 'Bells and lights.' For younger
audiences you could even make the shapes of lights and bells
as you say it.**

Lights and bells,
Bells and lights.
Cold pale mornings,
Long dark nights.
As winter's grey
Grabs hold and bites,
Christmas comes
With sounds and sights.
Lights and bells,
Bells and lights.

Lights and bells,
Bells and lights.
Angel songs,
Stars like kites.
Good News rings out
From Heaven's heights.
And Jesus comes
With sounds and sights.

Lights and bells,
Bells and lights.

Lights and bells.
Bells and lights.
Stable rafters
And starry brights
Paint shadow crosses
On wood uprights.
The baby turns...
Turns wrongs to rights.
Lights and bells,
Bells and lights.
For you and me
Turns wrongs to rights.
Lights and bells,
Bells and lights.

A Table Story

(Matthew 9:9-13)

Telling tips: It might be nice to sit behind a table to tell this one.
That way you'll have somewhere to put the story!

Matthew looked around the table and counted.

Ten guests.

Six dishes.

Five stacks of thin, flat bread.

And eight – no, nine – bottles of his best wine.

Matthew couldn't help himself. Counting was on his mind. Counting was in his blood. Counting was his business.

Counting. And tables.

Matthew had sat behind the one and done the other for as long as he could remember. Because counting was what a tax collector's job demanded.

So much for the masters back in Rome.

So much for the men who watched his back.

And so much, of course, for Matthew!

Matthew grinned as he remembered.

Count well, and you could count on a pretty good living. And if the taxpayers should complain, or the accountants in Rome grow suspicious, then you could usually fob them off with just a little more creative counting!

'A few more denarii, please!'

'Another pile of coins, sir!'

'Yes, that's right, ma'am, I need both of your chickens. It's hardly my fault that they're the last you've got.'

'Not enough! Not enough! Not enough!' That was his mantra. And his bully boys were always there to back up those words with a broken arm or a twisted neck. Was it any wonder then that he was hated and despised and left to socialize with the rest of society's outcasts?

Matthew looked around the table and counted. The table was full of outcasts. But how many of his friends had imagined that they would ever be sitting here?

Not Adam, for a start, Galilee's best brothel keeper. Nor Daniel, drunk from the day he could carry a bottle. Nor Caleb the conman. Nor Benjamin the womanizer. Nor Jacob the thief.

But here they were, eating and drinking and joking around with a rabbi, of all people! A rabbi, for heaven's sake! A rabbi!

It didn't add up.

No matter which way Matthew counted.

He'd never had any time for religion.

Dos and Don'ts.

Rights and Wrongs.

Following the rules. Keeping the traditions.

It was just another kind of counting, as far as he could tell.

The scribes and the priests and the Pharisees sat behind their tables too. They called them altars, of course, but it was just the same. And they stacked up good deeds and bad deeds as if they were piles of coins.

'Too much drink.'

'Too many women.'

'Too much gambling.'

'Too many lies.'

And in the end, when the counting was done, their answer was always the same.

'Not good enough! Not good enough! Not good enough!'

So what was the point? If he couldn't be good enough for them, how could he ever be good enough for God? Surely, then, it made sense to stay away from their tables altogether.

Yet, here he was, at the table with a rabbi.

Matthew looked around the table and counted.

There was not one of his friends that anyone would even think of calling good. They were rogues, one and all. Rogues, himself included. And not even lovable rogues!

They were dishonest, perverted, selfish and mean. But this rabbi was still sitting there among them.

And that's what counted the most.

Matthew's friends had all asked him, 'Why?'

'Why did you leave your job?'

'Why did you give up your fortune?'

'Why did you leave it all to follow him?'

And the answer was here – at the table.

Rabbi Jesus was a good man. Matthew had no doubt of that. But unlike so many other religious people whom Matthew had met, Jesus did not make his goodness an excuse for judgment.

He could be holy, somehow, without being holier-than-thou. He could eat with good people and bad people alike, and treat them all with respect, treat them all the same. And if that's what lay at the heart of this new kingdom that Jesus was always going on about, then Matthew wanted to be a part of it.

Because, when it came down to it, Matthew was tired of counting. Wherever he had been, whatever he had done, somebody was always counting.

Counting the taxes to see who owed the most.

Counting the profits to see who was the richest.

Counting the bad deeds to see who was the worst.

Counting the good deeds to see who was the purest.

But at this table – the table where Jesus sat – nobody was counting. And when nobody was counting, then everybody counted!

Good or bad. Rich or poor. Sinner or saint. God loved them all and welcomed them all to his table. Surely that's what Jesus was trying to say.

And as for change – changing to be more like Jesus? Yes, who wouldn't want to be like him? Love life as he did. See through the hypocrisy. Cut to the heart of things. Surely that invitation – to come and follow and be changed – was part of the equation as well.

Matthew looked around the table again. Looked at all his friends. Would they stay with Jesus? Would they follow? Would they change?

Matthew couldn't tell. But one thing he did know – there was no chance of them following Jesus without some kind of welcome in the first place.

Without his acceptance.

Without his invitation.

Without this table.

Two Answers

(Matthew 16:25)

Telling tips: You could use two people to tell this one. One could do
the Bible verse and the other could do the bits in between. Or you
could teach the Bible passage to your crowd and then lead them in
saying it at the appropriate times.

> Jesus said, 'Whoever wants to save his life will lose it,
> but whoever loses his life for me will find it.'

When I was at school, when I was only fifteen, one of my teachers
asked the class a question: 'What do you want to do with your life?'

> Jesus said, 'Whoever wants to save his life will lose it,
> but whoever loses his life for me will find it.'

The answers broke down into roughly two groups.
    Half of the class simply wanted to be happy.
    And the other half wanted to do something that would make the
world a better place.

> Jesus said, 'Whoever wants to save his life will lose it,
> but whoever loses his life for me will find it.'

Thirty years have passed.
    Thirty years and more.
    And I've watched my classmates.

And my friends.
And my family.
And my workmates.
And I've finally figured it out.
Only just figured it out.
Those weren't two answers.
Not two answers at all.
No, those answers were one and the same!

Jesus said, 'Whoever wants to save his life will lose it, but whoever loses his life for me will find it.'

Hey, That's OK!

(Matthew 18:21–35)

Telling tips: Divide your audience into two groups. Get one group to look at the other and say (with as much feeling as possible), 'I'm really sorry!' Then get the other group to respond to the first group (again with as much feeling as possible), 'Hey, that's OK!' Lead them in that every time it shows up in the text. It seems like a simple and almost silly device, but I can tell you that when I did this at one church, there were people in opposite groups who actually had fallen out with each other, so this became much more than a participation exercise.

Peter asked Jesus a question. 'If somebody hurts me,' he said, 'and then says, "I'm really sorry," how many times should I forgive them and say, "Hey, that's OK"?'

Before Jesus could answer, however, Peter offered an answer of his own. He thought it would sound good. He thought it would sound big-hearted. He thought it would be the kind of thing Jesus would like to hear.

'Should I forgive them... seven times?' said Peter.

(Do 'I'm really sorry!' and 'Hey, that's OK!' seven times)

It seemed like a lot of times to Peter, but Jesus was not impressed. Not at all.

'No,' answered Jesus. 'Not seven times. But *seventy times seven*!'

Peter did some quick maths. (Count on fingers) And somewhere on the way to 490, he ran out of fingers. That was a lot of times. Far more times than Peter had ever forgiven anybody.

So Jesus told him a story.

'Once upon a time there was a king,' said Jesus, 'and one of his servants owed him money.

'Not a little money. Not some money. Not even lots of money. But loads and loads and loads of money – a million pounds and more!

'The servant was brought before the king. And because the servant could not pay what he owed, the king commanded that the man, his wife and even his children be sold as slaves.

'The servant fell to his knees.

'"I'm really sorry!" he cried. "Be patient with me, please. Just give me another chance. And I promise I will pay back everything I owe."

'The king looked at his servant. He felt sorry for him. And then, much to the servant's surprise, the king smiled and said, "Hey, that's OK."

'Then he cancelled the debt, and set him free!

'The servant left the palace celebrating. And that's when he ran into another servant – a servant who owed HIM money.

'Not loads of money. Not a lot of money either. Just a little money, actually. A couple of quid – that's all.

'Did the first servant remember what the king had done for him? Not for a minute.

'He grabbed the second servant by the throat and demanded to be paid.

'So the second servant fell to his knees.

'"I'm really sorry!" he cried. "Be patient with me, please. Give me another chance and I will pay back everything I owe."

'But instead of saying, "Hey, that's OK," the first servant had the second servant thrown into jail.

'When the other servants heard about this, they told the king. And he was so angry that he had the first servant dragged before him again.

'"When you came to me and said, 'I'm really sorry,' I cancelled your debt and said, 'Hey, that's OK.'"

'"Why couldn't you do the same for someone else?"

'And with that, the king had the servant thrown into jail until he could repay the debt.

'Peter,' said Jesus. 'God is like that king.

'We say to him, "I'm really sorry" – more times than we can count. And even more times than that, he tells us, "Hey, that's OK." And all he really wants is for us to tell that to each other too.

'I'm really sorry,' said Peter. 'I didn't understand.'

And Jesus just smiled and said, 'Hey, that's OK.'

Feed the Poor

(Matthew 25:34–36)

**Telling tips: No specific tips here. Just be prepared for lots
of questions (and even more excuses) afterwards.**

'Feed the poor!' cried the vicar.

And the Lord said, 'Hey, I've got an idea! Why don't you sell the
churches? The market's strong. Prices are high. The places are
well-positioned. And besides, they're costing you an arm and a leg
to maintain!

'So why not sell them and give the money to the poor? You can
move into houses or schools or community centres. And if people
suggest that you're abandoning your legacy, just tell them that
your legacy has to do with restoring people, not twelfth-century
buildings!

'Go on. You can do it! Why ask someone else to pay the price?
Sell the churches and feed the poor. Because preaching about
sacrifice is not the same as making one.'

'Feed the poor!' cried the politician.

And the Lord said, 'Hey, I've got an idea! Why don't you raise
the taxes? I know it will make you unpopular and put your position
at risk. But isn't it time to be honest for a change? The only way to
feed the poor (and improve the hospitals and educate the children
and fix the infrastructure, now that I think of it) is to find the
money. And the only place to find it is from the people.

'This is about more than your image, more than the polls, more than New Labour or Compassionate Conservatism. So stop acting as if you care about the poor and do something to help them.

'Go on. You can do it. Why ask someone else to pay the price? Risk your position and raise the taxes. Because campaigning about sacrifice is not the same as making one.'

'Feed the poor!' cried the celebrity.

And the Lord said, 'Hey, I've got an idea! Why don't you put your hand into your own pocket? The poor know it's not Christmas time. There's nothing comical about the relief they need. And they still haven't found what they're looking for.

'And that's because, in spite of your good intentions, you still live like kings while much of the world starves. So instead of begging the guy who stocks the shelves at Tesco's to give another fiver, why not forego that next Ferrari, or that third country house, or that million-pound wedding? And meet the needs of the poor yourself.

'Go on. You can do it. Why ask someone else to pay the price? You could cancel the debts of some developing nations with a stroke of your own pen. Because singing about sacrifice is not the same as making one.

'Feed the poor!' cried the people.

And the Lord said, 'Hey, I've got an idea! Why don't you re-mortgage your house? It's worth – what? – five, ten, twenty times what you paid for it? That's money you didn't earn. It's just come your way. So why not take out a second mortgage, and instead of adding that conservatory or taking that "holiday of a lifetime", why not give the money away? Go on. You can do it. Why leave it to someone else? Because hoping for sacrifice isn't the same as making one.'

'Feed the poor,' wrote the author.

And the Lord said, 'Hey, I've got an idea! You know those royalties you're getting for this book...?'

And that's when the author put down his pen.

The Tree of Life *or* A Tale of Three More Trees

(Genesis 3, Matthew 27)

Telling tips: No advice really, just one for you to tell.

And the angel who guarded the gates of Eden took one last look at Adam. He burned those features for ever in his mind – sad eyes, sorry brow, the face of loneliness and rejection – then raised his fiery sword into the sky. And there he remained, blocking the entrance to the Garden and the path to the Tree of Life.

Age after age, he stood at his post, the beauty of the Garden all about him. He knew its smell and its taste and its sounds, but he had no time to enjoy it. For all he could do was watch, in case the face of Adam should return.

And perhaps that is why, one day, the impossible finally happened.

It wasn't a sound that caught his attention. It was more like a feeling. A sense, deep inside the angel, that something was wrong. And that is why he lowered his sword, turned and ran through the Garden. And that is how he discovered that the Tree of Life was gone!

Only a ragged hole remained, as if the tree had been torn out by its roots. The angel drove his sword into the ground, its flaming orange dimmed to a flickering blue. Then he knelt beside it and buried his face in his hands.

What was he going to do? Guarding the tree had been his

responsibility. But somehow he had failed. And there was only one course of action he could take: he must find the Tree of Life and watch over it once again.

So like Adam before him, he walked sadly out of the Garden of Eden. But he did not wander over the unplowed wilderness of the world. No, he opened his wings and flung himself through the fabric of time and space – in search of the Tree of Life.

There was a smell to Paradise – a purity, a freshness – which he was certain he could recognize. And so he sniffed his way through aeons and epochs until, finally, he picked up the scent. Then he raised his sword and sliced his way into one particular time and place.

The air was cold, the clouds icy with the promise of winter. Below the clouds there were hills, mile after mile of them, portioned off by rivers and valleys. And trees? There were more trees than the angel had ever seen. But they were stripped bare of leaves. All but one, that is, whose pointed branches burned bright from the window of a single house. That was the one he headed for, until his senses picked up something else – chimney smoke and the sound of human voices.

'Adam!' the angel cursed, as he flew, invisible, into the house and hovered next to a small plastic replica of himself.

Adams were everywhere below, their hands full of bright and shiny things. The angel looked long and hard, but he could find no one who resembled the sad Adam he had chased from the Garden.

Instead, these Adams were laughing – big ones and little ones, brown ones and pale ones – all together. Then finally, they settled themselves on the furniture and on the floor, and one of the Adams spoke.

'Let us give thanks to God!' he said. 'For the gift of his son, for the gifts we hold in our hands, and for the gifts we are to each other.'

That is when a voice whispered to the angel from among the bright branches. 'I am not the tree you seek,' it said. 'I am the Tree of Laughter. Where sadness turns to joy, where tears give way to smiles, where all that oppresses or frightens is conquered by hope and peace, that is where you will find me. But you must look elsewhere if you would find the Tree of Life.'

And so the angel left the Tree of Laughter, and the merrymakers gathered in its shade, and burst the curtain of time once more – in search of the Tree of Life.

It was not long before he caught the scent again. So he pulled out his sword and slashed a path into another place.

The sun was red against the horizon – red as the angel's sword – and it burned the land brown and bare. Except for one tree, that is, whose leaves hung cool and green over the banks of a sleepy river.

There were noises beneath this tree as well. Strange, muffled sounds – human sounds that made the angel cautious.

'Adam!' he whispered, and invisible once more, he hovered closer to have a look.

They were Adams, certainly – a male and a female, skin black as the river's edge. And they were holding one another and caressing one another and pressing their lips together. And then they just sat there and stared at each other and said nothing for hours and hours. Nothing at all.

'I am not the tree you seek,' the branches quivered at last. 'I am the Tree of Love. Watch and you will see.'

And in a moment, the sun rose and fell, thousands upon thousands of times! The two Adams became four, then ten, then a hundred. Their hair bleached white, their bodies bent and stooped, and they held children and grandchildren and great-grandchildren in their ever-more-feeble arms. But they never grew tired of staring into each other's eyes and saying nothing for hours. Nothing at all.

'Where there is tenderness,' the tree continued. 'Where there is commitment and kindness and passion, that is where you will find me. But you must look elsewhere if you would find the Tree of Life.'

And so the angel resumed his search, determined that he would not be foiled again. This time, however, the scent was nowhere to be found. He had almost given up hope, in fact, when he smelled it – the faintest odour of Paradise. Skeptical, he stopped and sniffed, and the longer he waited, the stronger the scent became. The Tree of Life was near. He was sure of it. So he drew his sword and ripped, one more time, through the fabric of heaven and earth.

And immediately, he was sorry that he had.

The sky shuddered dark around him. Thunder clapped. A fierce wind blew. And below all was lifeless and grey. Surely he had made another mistake.

But the scent was stronger than ever. So he plunged, invisible, towards the earth. And all at once, he knew. He was in the right place after all. For there, on a hill, stood Adam!

Sad eyes. Sorry brow. The face of loneliness and rejection. He would recognize those features anywhere!

'Adam!' he bellowed. 'Adam!' he cursed. 'What have you done with the Tree of Life?'

But Adam would not answer. His head lolled heavily to one side. His lips were blistered and bruised.

'He cannot hear you,' whispered a voice. 'He hears no one. He is dead.'

'Dead?' the angel wondered. 'Adam? Dead?'

'Not Adam,' the voice replied. 'But Adam's son. And the Son of God as well. Sent by the Maker himself to undo Adam's damage and repair the path to Paradise.'

'And who... who are you?' the angel asked. But there was no need to wait for an answer. All he had to do was look – beyond the face, beyond the hands, beyond the outstretched arms of the man before him. And, sure enough, there was wood. Wood cut and shaped. Wood hammered and pierced. Wood stripped bare of all beauty and blossom and life.

'No!' the angel cried, falling to his knees. 'This is not possible. Who could have done this to you?'

'The Maker of all things,' the voice said softly. 'It was he who plucked me from the Garden. He who brought me here. He who planted me in this place. For where evil is overwhelmed by goodness, where failure is comforted by grace, where sins are forgiven and debts are repaid and darkness is blinded by light, that is where you will find me. For I am what the Maker always intended me to be. I am the Tree of Life.'

'And what about me?' the angel pleaded. 'What am I to do now? What am I to be?'

'What the Maker made you for,' answered the fading voice.

And so the angel climbed slowly to his feet and, with his sword raised like lightning to the sky, stood guard on the hill of death and watched over the Tree of Life.

The Apostle Paul and
Sir Isaac Newton

(Matthew 28, Luke 24, John 20, 1 Corinthians 15)

Telling tips: Again just another one to tell on your own.

The tomb was sealed.
But the tomb couldn't hold him.

The guards were armed.
But the guards couldn't hold him.

Three days had passed.
But time couldn't hold him.

The man was dead.
But death couldn't hold him.

Mary Magdalene tried.
But she couldn't hold him.

The door was shut.
But the room couldn't hold him.

And when he walked to the top of the hill
And bid his friends goodbye, gravity,
Even gravity could not hold him.

So how come we can hold him
Closer than a brother?
How come we can hold him
Where two or three are gathered?

Death has been swallowed up in victory.
That's how.
And even gravity is no match for love.

Jesus' Media Consultant

(Mark 1:21–39)

Telling tips: This is another story for two tellers. The person reading the Bible passage needs to read it well, but the media consultant should be a bit of an actor. The script can go on a clipboard, of course – the only prop you'll need – unless you've got a laptop or an organizer you can use.

They went to Capernaum, and when the Sabbath came...

Jesus' media consultant said, 'We've got an 11 o'clock at the synagogue, Rabbi. There's time for a little teaching, a little healing – but you'll have to make it quick. We've got a full schedule today.'

Jesus went into the synagogue and began to teach. The people were amazed at his teaching, because he taught them as one who had authority, not as the teachers of the Law.

Just then a man in their synagogue who was possessed by an evil spirit cried out, 'What do you want with us, Jesus of Nazareth? Have you come to destroy us? I know who you are – the Holy One of God!'

And Jesus' media consultant said, 'A heckler! That's the last thing we need. Do something, quick!'

'Be quiet!' said Jesus sternly. 'Come out of him!'

The evil spirit shook the man violently and came out of him with a shriek.

The people were all so amazed that they asked each other, 'What is this? A new teaching – and with authority! He even gives orders to evil spirits and they obey him.'

'That was quick thinking,' said Jesus' media consultant. 'It could have been a disaster, but now I think we can use it to our advantage. I've got some friends in the local press. I'll make a few calls.'

News about him spread quickly over the whole region of Galilee.
As soon as they left the synagogue...

Jesus' media consultant said, 'We have a light lunch scheduled next. At the home of a local businessman called Simon. I think he has something to do with the fishing industry.'

They went with James and John to the home of Simon and Andrew. Simon's mother-in-law was in bed with a fever and they told Jesus about her.

'Not good,' said Jesus' media consultant. 'This is going to put us way behind schedule. I say we get out as quick as we can and grab something on the way. Burgers. A kebab. What do you think?'

So Jesus went to her, took her hand and helped her up.
The fever left her and she began to wait on them.

'I've got to hand it to you,' said Jesus' media consultant. 'You know how to get yourself out of a difficult situation. I would never have thought of that. But we're gonna have to hurry. I've got several more appearances scheduled for today. There's a five o'clock, a six o'clock, and an eight o'clock if we can squeeze it in.'

That evening after sunset the people brought to Jesus all the sick and demon-possessed. The whole town gathered at the door...

'Male, female. Gen X, Gen Y!' said Jesus' media consultant. 'I like the demographics!'

And Jesus healed many who had various diseases. He also drove out many demons, but he would not let the demons speak because they knew who he was.

'I want you to get a good night's sleep,' said Jesus' media consultant. 'It looks as if we've got a long day ahead of us tomorrow. We can't let this momentum slip. These people are just itching for more!'

Very early in the morning, while it was still dark, Jesus got up, left the house and went off to a solitary place, where he prayed.

'So where'd he go?' shouted Jesus' media consultant. 'Talk to me, people! We've got briefings and meetings scheduled here. We're on the edge of something big. This is not a good time for the rabbi to freak out on us!'

Simon and his companions went to look for him, and when they found him, they exclaimed: 'Everyone is looking for you!'

Jesus' media consultant exclaimed too. 'Praying? What do you mean, you've been praying? We've got make-up in ten minutes. And a list of appearances as long as my arm. This is important stuff,

Rabbi. Another day in this town and I think this messiah thing of yours will go right through the roof.'

Jesus replied, 'Let us go somewhere else – to the nearby villages – so that I can preach there also. That is why I have come.'

'Somewhere else?' cried Jesus' media consultant. 'When this place is ripe for the picking? What about the schedule? What about the appointments? We've got a slot on Oprah, for goodness' sake! What am I supposed to tell her – that you can't come on because you PRAYED?'

So Jesus travelled throughout Galilee, preaching in their synagogues and driving out demons.

And Jesus' media consultant? He packed up his laptop and went home.

A Little Shining,
a Little Sowing

Mark 4:21–32

Telling tips: You might want to teach everyone the chorus first, or put it up on a screen. It works very nicely with a few simple actions.

'A little shining' – hands open beside face in a glowing motion.

'A little sowing' – pretend to toss seeds in a sowing motion.

'The kingdom of God keeps growing and growing' – arms outstretched, wider and wider, or above head, taller and taller, in a growing motion.

A little shining, a little sowing,
the kingdom of God keeps growing and growing.

'If you have a lamp,' said Jesus, 'you've got to let it glow. Under a bowl. Under the bed. It's no use there at all! But put it on a lampstand – for everyone to see – and all that once was hidden is revealed!

'If you have a lamp,' said Jesus, 'you've got to let it glow.'

A little shining, a little sowing,
the kingdom of God keeps growing and growing.

'If you have a seed,' said Jesus, 'you've got to let it go. Drop it into the ground. That's your part, and God will do the rest. Seed to stem. Stem to stalk. Stalk to bushy head. You couldn't make it happen if you tried.

'If you have a seed,' said Jesus, 'you've got to let it go.'

80

A little shining, a little sowing,
the kingdom of God keeps growing and growing.

'So plant your seed,' said Jesus, 'then stand back and watch it grow!
A mustard seed is small. The smallest seed of all. But it grows into
a great big bushy...bush! With great big bushy branches for birds
to roost and rest. So plant your seed,' said Jesus, 'then stand back
and watch it grow!'

A little shining, a little sowing,
the kingdom of God keeps growing and growing.

The Dazzler

(Mark 9:2–13)

Telling tips: You might want to teach your crowd a few actions to go along with the 'p' words. On 'puffing' get them to huff and puff. On 'petrified', get them to shriek. On 'peaceful' get them to sigh, 'Ahhh'. And on 'puzzled' get them to scratch their heads and say, 'Huh?'

Peter was puffing! Huffing and puffing! He and Jesus and James and John had just walked up a mountain. But before he could catch his breath, something strange happened. Something he'd never expected. Jesus started to shine. That's right – shine! And his clothes were like an advertisement for some brand new laundry powder – brighter than any bleach could make them!

And that's not all. Moses was standing there with him! Moses, who had led God's people out of slavery!

And Elijah – the prophet who stood up to King Ahab and faced down the prophets of Baal – was there too! Even though he and Moses had been dead for hundreds of years!

Now Peter was petrified! Really petrified! What could he say? What could he do? So he just blurted out the first thing that popped into his head.

'Jesus!' he stammered. 'Why don't we put up three shelters, three tents, three tabernacles? One for you and one for Moses and one for Elijah, to savour this special moment.

And that's when the cloud appeared. A cloud that surrounded

them all. And out of the cloud came a voice. And Peter was more petrified than ever.

'This is my Son!' said the voice. And there was no mistaking whose voice it was. 'This is my Son whom I love. Listen to him!'

And then as suddenly as everything had happened, it was over. Jesus was standing alone.

So Peter was peaceful. Peaceful at last. And then Jesus led them back down the mountain. 'I don't want you to mention this to anyone,' he said. 'Keep it to yourselves until after I have come back from the dead.'

Now Peter was puzzled. Really puzzled. 'Back from the dead?' he wondered. 'What does Jesus mean by that?' And James and John wondered too. But the question troubled them so much that they decided to ask a different question instead.

'Why do the teachers of the Law say that Elijah must come before the messiah?'

'Elijah has come,' said Jesus. 'Just as the scriptures said he would. Just as they also said that the Messiah must suffer and be rejected.'

And even though they were now more puzzled than ever, Peter and James and John dared ask no more. And they walked down the mountain in silence.

Drinking and Dunking

(Mark 10:35–45)

Telling tips: You could get a couple of volunteers to play James and John and come up around you. Then just get them to say the lines. The congregation could be the rest of the disciples. Teach them their lines ahead of time.

James walked up to Jesus and stood on his right side.

John walked up to Jesus and stood on his left.

Then the brothers each put an arm around Jesus' shoulders and whispered so that no one else could hear.

'Jesus, we'd like to ask a favour. When you finally set up your kingdom, and sit down upon your throne...'

'Could I have the throne on your right side?' asked James.

'And could I,' asked John, 'have the throne on your left?'

Jesus didn't know whether to laugh or cry. These two were his closest disciples. Yet their question showed that they understood so little of what he'd tried to teach them.

'You don't realize what you're asking for,' he said at last. And then, like any good teacher, he followed their question with a question of his own.

'Can you drink the cup I drink?' he asked. 'Can you join me in my baptism?'

James and John glanced at each other. They were strange questions. But drinking and dunking seemed a small price to pay for the chance to reign in Jesus' kingdom.

'Of course we can,' they whispered back.

And Jesus just sighed. For he knew the cup was a poisoned chalice, and his baptism was a drowning pool. Death was the only way to the kingdom. A cross, the path to the throne. And despite their innocence and lack of understanding, Jesus knew that his friends would walk that path too.

'You will drink my cup,' he sighed again. 'You will join me in my baptism too. But as for thrones – that's not my decision to make.'

James and John wanted to know more. But before they could ask, their secret meeting was interrupted by the other ten disciples.

Someone had been listening in. Or maybe James and John were just lousy whisperers. But a chorus of 'Oi' and 'What's going on here?' and 'Hey, I wanted that throne!' was finally brought to an end by Jesus.

'Listen. Listen. Listen!' he said. And he wasn't whispering now. 'You lot seem awfully interested in thrones. Fear, power, position and authority, that's how those who sit on them get their way. That's how they show their greatness. And I'm here to tell you that it must not work that way among you!

'In my kingdom, the slave will be master and the servant will sit on the throne. And greatness will be measured by how well you give yourselves to one another. For even I did not come to be pampered and preened and catered for, but to live as a servant and die as one too – to give myself up as a ransom for the world.'

'Drinking and dunking,' James whispered to John.

'Drinking and dunking and dying,' John whispered back.

And there were no further questions about thrones.

A Christmas Eve Service for Those Who Don't Feel Like Celebrating

(Luke 2)

Telling tips: My dad passed away in the autumn of 2002, and by the time Christmas came around, I didn't feel much like celebrating. So I put this collection of readings together on the assumption that I probably wasn't alone – that there were others in the church who had felt or were feeling or would one day feel just like me. I just put in what seemed to be appropriate songs and carols and prayers between the readings. You can do the same if you like.

Every now and then, I read a familiar passage from the Bible, and something strikes me for the very first time. A line I've never really heard before – or never really thought about. There's a line like that at the end of the passage that we're going to focus on now. I'd like you to listen for it as I read Luke 2:8–18. (*Read Luke 2:8-18 NIV*)

The shepherds spread the word. They went and told people what they had seen and heard. Friends. Relations. Citizens of Bethlehem. And when those people heard the story, they were amazed. Well, who wouldn't be?

But were they moved? Convinced? Or changed? That's a different thing altogether, isn't it? And it's true for us as well.

Because sometimes, even though it's Christmas – maybe even

the first Christmas – we're just not in a Christmas-y mood. We just don't feel like celebrating.

The shepherds' first port of call is the local pub. 'Bethlehem's Best' – that's the brew they serve. And while the punters sit and sip, the shepherds tell their story.

There's a lot of ooh-ing and aah-ing and 'Never!' But when the shepherds repeat the angels' message – 'good news of great joy!' – a man in the corner grunts and gulps down what's left of his pint. He's a merchant, travelling up and down the land of Palestine and beyond. And he knows, because he's seen it, that good news is in very short supply.

Famine to the east. Rebellion to the west. Higher taxes and even higher crime. Hospital queues. Inadequate transport. Falling pensions. Failing schools.

And, just like us, he wonders: How do you do it? How do you celebrate good news – how do you even believe in the possibility – when all the news you hear is bad?

So let's light a candle. And let's pray. For every one who wonders with him. For everyone this Christmas who struggles to believe that the news – any news – can be good.

'Good news of great joy!' the shepherds repeat. And they're standing on the tables now and flapping pretend wings!

Some punters laugh. Some punters cheer. But the barmaid turns round and wipes her eyes with a dirty towel. Her husband is out of work. One of her children is seriously ill. And just last week, her grandmother died. Everything seems to be falling apart. Everywhere she looks is dark. She wants to share the shepherds' excitement – or at least she feels she should. But she can't. Not now. Because everything is still too painful, too close, too hopeless, too sad.

And just like us – because we've been there, or one day will be – just like us she wonders: How do you sing 'Joy to the World' when all you feel is sadness?

So let's light a candle. And let's pray a prayer. For everyone who wonders with her. For everyone this Christmas who's sad.

The shepherds are in full swing now. And even though they can't begin to sound like angels, the message is the same. 'Glory to God in the highest. And peace to people on earth.'

One punter has had enough. It's not just their singing he can't stand. Nor the disruption of a quiet night's drink. It's that line that galls.

'Peace on earth,' he mutters. And he slams the door on his way out. 'Peace on earth? While the Romans rule over us? While they crush us and control us and lay claim to God's own land? Peace on earth? Impossible!'

And surely we wonder with him.

Afghanistan and Iraq. Korea and Africa. India and Pakistan.

And Israel. Still Israel. Always Israel.

How can we possibly sing about peace on earth, when the world is on the brink of war?

So let's light a candle. And let's pray a prayer. In the hope that, one Christmas, the angels' song might come true.

The shepherds' tale is almost done. But the punters are losing interest. Angels are one thing – strange, exotic, amazing! But a baby? Everyone's seen a baby. And so the end of the story is a bit of a dud.

But it's also the beginning of an answer. The answer to all we have felt and worried over and wondered about. You see, Christmas promises are one thing. Sometimes, by God's grace, they come true. And sometimes, foiled by man's stubbornness and sin, they fall short. Their complete fulfilment lies ahead – in the kingdom to come.

Christmas promises are one thing. But a Christmas present is something else. For God's gift to us is God himself. God in a very specific way:

God in a manger.

God in a stable.

God vulnerable and fragile and small.

God like us, in fact.

God with us in the bad news.

God with us in the sadness.

God with us when we cry for peace.

God with us when the promises come true.

And God with us when they don't.

God in a cradle. And God on a cross.

God puts himself in our hands. To suckle and to nurture. To receive or to reject.

God's gift is God himself.

So let's light a candle. And let's pray a prayer for everyone who wants God's gift this Christmas. For everyone who longs for God himself.

Mary Went Looking
for Jesus

(Luke 2:41–50, John 19:25)

**Telling tips: Here's another one just for you to read. You might
want to start with a Bible in your hand. You can read out the Luke 2
passage. It will help the sense later.**

> **Every year his parents went to Jerusalem for the Feast of
> the Passover. When Jesus was twelve years old, they went
> up to the Feast, according to the custom. After the Feast
> was over, while his parents were returning home, the boy
> Jesus stayed behind in Jerusalem, but they were unaware
> of it. Thinking he was in their company, they travelled on
> for a day. Then they began looking for him among their
> relatives and friends. When they did not find him, they
> went back to Jerusalem to look for him.**

Mary went looking for Jesus. Her heart was pounding, her hands
sweating. She hadn't seen him for days.

Mary went looking for Jesus. 'Have you seen my son?' she asked.
'Have you seen my son? My boy?'

Mary went looking for Jesus. The hot wind biting her face, chasing
the tears from the corners of her eyes.

Mary went looking for Jesus. Up and down, and in and out, the crowded streets of Jerusalem.

Mary went looking for Jesus. And suddenly she remembered: The same search. The same crowded streets. But, oh, so long ago.

Mary went looking for Jesus. And finally she found him. But it wasn't like that other time. Not at all.

Then, she had looked down at his twelve-year-old face. Now, she was forced to look up.

Then, the temple teachers had praised him, amazed! Now, they shouted and swore.

Then, his face was adolescent fresh. Now, it was covered in blood.

Mary went looking for Jesus. 'Why are you looking for me?' he'd asked. And he'd fixed her with a look both innocent and wise. A look that said: 'I'm sorry you're worried. I know what I'm doing. Everything will be all right.

'Didn't you know that I'd be here in my Father's house, doing my Father's will?'

Mary went looking for Jesus. He was looking at her now as well. And it was the same look. The very same look. The bright boy. The dying man. 'I'm sorry you're worried. I know what I'm doing. Everything will be all right.'

They say you never stop being your mother's son.

Or your father's either, I guess.

Mary went looking for Jesus. And she found him in a temple. And she found him on a cross. Where she always knew he'd be – doing his Father's will.

Bzz-y

(Luke 10:38–42)

Telling tips: Teach the chorus to your crowd first of all. (They'll be repeating it a lot!) Then do it more and more quickly as the story progresses. Get them huffing and puffing (like Martha!), and then contrast that with a slow, deliberate reading of Jesus' words at the end.

Busy, busy, busy,
Busy as a bee.
Martha was so busy,
She could hardly even breathe!
(x2)

Wash the dishes, cook the meals,
Put the kettle on.
Clean the windows, sweep the floor,
Work is never done!

Busy, busy, busy,
Busy as a bee.
Martha was so busy,
She could hardly even breathe!
(x2)

Jesus came to visit once,
She put on such a spread!

Home-made bread and fancy cakes
And pickled chicken heads.

Busy, busy, busy,
Busy as a bee.
Martha was so busy,
She could hardly even breathe!
(x2)

'I do all the work,' she moaned,
'It all comes down to me!
While sister Mary chats with Jesus
Idle and carefree.'

Busy, busy, busy,
Busy as a bee.
Martha was so busy,
She could hardly even breathe!
(x2)

'Slow down, Martha,' Jesus smiled.
'Take it easy, please.
Hospitality is good,
But you still need time to breathe.
Time to think and time to pray,
Time to spend with me.
So join your sister Mary,
And then we'll sort out tea.'

Busy, busy, busy,
Busy as a bee.
So Martha sat and listened
And at last found time to breathe!

Untie the Ox

(Luke 13:10–17)

Telling tips: Divide your crowd into two groups. Get one group to say 'Untie the ox' and the other to say 'And set the woman free!' Then lead them in that chorus at the end of each line, making it bigger and bigger as you go.

Jesus was teaching in the synagogue.
Untie the ox and set the woman free!

When he spotted a woman, her back bent double.
Untie the ox and set the woman free!

He called her forward. He laid his hands on her.
Untie the ox and set the woman free!

She stood up straight and gave thanks to God!
Untie the ox and set the woman free!

But the ruler of the synagogue was angry and indignant.
Untie the ox and set the woman free!

'You've healed on the Sabbath! You've broken our laws!'
Untie the ox and set the woman free!

'There are six days for healing. Do it in your own time!'
Untie the ox and set the woman free!

But Jesus just sighed and shook his head.
Untie the ox and set the woman free!

'You hypocrites,' he muttered. 'You hypocrites!' he cried.
Untie the ox and set the woman free!

'You'd loose an ox and lead it to the water.'
Untie the ox and set the woman free!

'You'd do it on the sabbath and think nothing of it!'
Untie the ox and set the woman free!

'So why not the same for this daughter of Abraham?'
Untie the ox and set the woman free!

'Why not the same for this daughter of Abraham?'
Untie the ox and set the woman free!

'So why not show mercy to this daughter of Abraham?'
Untie the ox and set the woman free!

Bound by ropes and bound by illness.
Untie the ox and set the woman free!

Bound by rules and regulations.
Untie the ox and set the woman free!

Bound by tradition, bound by theology.
Untie the ox and set the woman free!

Bound by institutions, bound by bureaucracy.
Untie the ox and set the woman free!

Bound by everything but mercy.
Untie the ox and set the woman free!

So let's follow the one who died on the cross.
Untie the ox and set the woman free!

And set us free by his pain and loss.
Untie the ox and set the woman free!

Let's untie the ox and set the woman free!
Let's untie the ox and set the woman free!
Let's untie the ox and set the woman free!

Because that's what it means to live in Jesus' community.

Untie the Ox (Again)

(Luke 13:10–17)

**Telling tips: This is just another take on the same passage, but
I enjoyed writing both treatments of this text, and thought you
might enjoy them both as well. Suffice it to say that this needs to
be read in a very officious manner.**

My Dear Eli,

As a fellow Pharisee, you have asked for my reaction to the
incident at the synagogue this past sabbath, and I ask, in turn, for
your patience and understanding, because my answer may not be
exactly what you wanted to hear.

The facts are clear enough. I was, as you know, present myself
and witnessed all that was said and done.

The rabbi, Jesus, was teaching. The nature of his discourse is not
relevant to the issue at hand. Suffice it to say that he is, as many
have already noted, a clear and intelligent communicator, who
appeals to the educated and the uninformed alike.

He was in the middle of his message when he noticed the old
woman. As far as I could tell, she made no effort to attract his
attention (and is therefore, in my opinion, innocent of any
wrongdoing with regard to the subsequent violation of the sabbath
Law). No, I think it is fair to say that HE spotted HER – bent over
nearly double with some affliction or other.

I have, by the way, attempted to ascertain the exact nature of her
infirmity. While there are many opinions on the matter – ranging
from some birth defect, on the one hand, to the influence of

demonic powers, on the other – there is no question that the woman was genuinely ill, and not, as some of our more cynical colleagues have suggested, a 'plant'.

So, Jesus spotted this woman. And interrupting his own discourse, he invited her to come forward. To be honest, I would have thought that this was the time for the ruler of the synagogue to act. It was a highly irregular and uncomfortable moment, not in keeping with the usual order and decorum of the service. Had I been in his position, I would have sent the woman back straight away, and all would have ended happily. As it was, he failed to exercise his responsibility at this juncture, and the woman responded to Jesus' invitation.

'Woman,' he said – so that everyone could hear, 'Woman, you are set free from your infirmity.' Then he laid his hands on her, and immediately she stood up straight and gave thanks to God for her healing.

It was at this point that the ruler of the synagogue finally decided to act. And his timing could not have been worse. The crowd was understandably impressed, indeed, excited by what had happened, and were in sympathy with the woman and her plight. Yes, the Law had been violated. There is no question of that. And, yes, something needed to be done. But this was not exactly what you might call 'a teachable moment'.

Playing right into Jesus' hands (more on this later), he rose with great indignation and tactlessly suggested that the sick should seek healing not on the sabbath but on the other six days when it was allowed. This produced an angry murmur from the crowd – rightly, I think, because it placed the blame on the sick woman and not on Jesus, who, as I have already said, was clearly at fault for instigating this situation in the first place.

Perhaps the ruler of the synagogue aimed his comments at the woman because he was afraid to attack Jesus directly. We are all aware, by now, of his combative reputation where matters of the Law are concerned. But the ploy failed miserably, and Jesus launched into yet another of his famous invectives against hypocrisy and the keeping of the Law.

We have heard it all before: 'Whitewashed tombs, dirty bowls, murderers of the prophets, etcetera and so forth, blah, blah, blah...' But I must say that on this particular occasion, he argued his point rather well.

Jesus compared the loosing of the woman from her illness to the loosing of an ox or an ass from its stall.

'If an animal needs to drink,' he suggested, 'the sabbath law permits us to do what little work is necessary to untie it and lead it to water. And therefore,' he argued, 'Why should we not also be permitted to do what work is necessary to loose a woman from her infirmity?'

You and I, of course, can see the flaws in this argument immediately. Scholars have debated for centuries over the nature of the knots, the effort involved in the untying, and the distance to the water. The situation is nowhere near as clear-cut as Jesus suggested.

But my point is that, to the untrained mind – and I mean no disrespect here, but that would include the bulk of the congregation in the synagogue that day – Jesus' argument would seem quite plausible.

It certainly convinced THAT crowd, and the upshot was their overwhelming approval for what Jesus had done and abuse and scorn for those of us who see things in a more scripturally exact light.

So what is to be done? That was your question. And here, as promised, is my answer.

Nothing.

I told you, you wouldn't like it. But I am totally convinced that it is the right course. I know what many of our colleagues have said. I have heard plans to challenge him, debate with him, even trump up charges against him. But these are either useless or unethical or both.

The very incident that we are considering is a perfect illustration of my point. Confrontation is counterproductive. The best thing is to do nothing – and wait!

Follow me for just a moment here. Have we not dealt with movements and splits and sects in the past? Everything from serious ascetics like the Essenes to that ridiculous Braying Brotherhood of Balaam's Ass? Do you remember? Palm-frond ears tied to their heads. Rope tails hanging from behind. All in the hope that an hour's hee-hawing would result in some word of prophecy!

It still makes me shudder to think about it. But what did we do? We waited – that's what – and let the weight of time and institution and regulation and rule bring these groups back to their senses. And so now the Essenes are quietly at work in the desert, and, the last I heard, the few remaining Braying Brothers had composed a thoughtful commentary on the care and feeding of donkeys – all thoughts of prophecy and hee-hawing banished for ever.

We waited. It worked. And that is why I say we do the same with Jesus.

His group is small now. He can move freely among them, tailoring his teaching to their daily needs and changing situations. They don't need rules. He is there, beside them, to answer any question, to advise on any problem.

But the success of his movement will create a whole new dynamic!

'Success?' I hear you say. 'Success is the last thing we want!'

But hear me out. Success means growth. Not one band of disciples travelling from place to place, but lots of little bands who will have to settle eventually into communities of some kind or other. Communities dotted, here and there, all over our land.

Will Jesus be able to advise them daily in that situation? Of course not. There will need to be rules to govern their behaviour, regulations to order their communities, structures to provide leadership. And inevitably, there will be discussions and debates over the nature of all of these. And, in the midst of that, they are sure to forget all about their 'radical agenda', their newfound 'freedom', and, best of all, their criticism of us!

Inside information that I am privy to suggests that there have already been questions.

Jesus says that we must love our neighbour.

'Who exactly is my neighbour?' someone asks.

Jesus says that we must forgive.

'How many times?' That's what one of his followers wants to know.

You can already imagine the commentaries, the scholarly debate and the regulations that will arise from just these two issues.

Don't you see, Eli? It's inevitable. There is no other way.

Rules. Regulations.

Committees. Commentaries.

Bureaucracy. Hypocrisy!

And quicker than you can say, 'The Braying Brotherhood of Balaam's Ass', the followers of Jesus will be sitting where we're sitting now!

I ask you, what is the alternative? Unless Jesus can find some way to spirit himself from group to group, here and there and everywhere, he will no longer be able to advise his followers personally on how they should follow his teaching. And what happens when he dies? What choice will they have then but to enshrine his words in some kind of fixed rule? And then who will help them apply and interpret? Jesus is not likely to live for ever, is he?

So let's wait. Time and human nature and the grinding process of institutionalization are on our side. And it won't be long until someone stands up in the midst of Jesus' followers, cries, 'Hypocrite!' and asks why they put their own rules and traditions above some basic human need.

Thank you for patiently wading through this lengthy epistle. I hope that you can see my point, or, at the very least, would be happy to engage in further discussion on this matter – perhaps at the next meeting of the Kid Boiled in its Mother's Milk Exclusionary Subcommittee.

But in the meantime, let us wait. Just wait. For I am confident that this approach will do more to slow the progress of Jesus' movement than anything else we could imagine.

All the best, then.

Your brother and friend,

The Pharisee, Matathias

Count the Cost

Luke 14:25–35

Telling tips: I wrote this originally for the final worship service at a week of Spring Harvest and have adapted it for more general use. As with many of the other readings in the book, you will need to teach your group the chorus before you start. You can either get them to count on their fingers (lots of fun!) or if it's a more mathematically advanced bunch, they could do it in their heads (frankly, not so much fun!). The chorus has a nice rhythm to it, which you can get them to practice and emphasize. And because it is repeated so often, you might want to make it 'bigger' each time.

1, 2, 3, 4, 5, 6, 7.
Count the cost. Count the cost.
Count the cost in the kingdom of heaven.

Once there was a large group of people following Jesus.

A large group at church on Sunday. A large group at a conference. A large group on retreat perhaps. Who knows?

But a large group of people who'd just had an important and significant time and were feeling really close to Jesus.

1, 2, 3, 4, 5, 6, 7.
Count the cost. Count the cost.
Count the cost in the kingdom of heaven.

So Jesus turned to them and shared a few hard truths about the journey home.

Not the congestion. Not the road works. Not the food at the service stations. But the journey after that – the following days and weeks and months.

1, 2, 3, 4, 5, 6, 7.
Count the cost. Count the cost.
Count the cost in the kingdom of heaven.

'If you want to follow me,' said Jesus, 'you will have to hate your father, your mother; your husband, your wife; your brother, your sister; your child, your own life.'

Now, the people had been on trips with their families before, and they figured that this was likely to happen at some point on the way home, in any case.

So Jesus continued.

1, 2, 3, 4, 5, 6, 7.
Count the cost. Count the cost.
Count the cost in the kingdom of heaven.

'And if you want to be my disciple,' he said, 'you will have to pick up your cross and follow me.'

This was getting more serious!

'You wouldn't build a house,' he said, 'or a garage, or anything, without first working out the price. What if you could only afford the concrete slab floor and then had to stop? Imagine how the neighbours would laugh!

'Or what if you were a king, about to fight a battle. You had ten thousand soldiers and your enemy had twice that number. You'd think long and hard about it, wouldn't you? And try to find a peaceful solution if you didn't think you could see it through.'

1, 2, 3, 4, 5, 6, 7.
Count the cost. Count the cost.
Count the cost in the kingdom of heaven.

'Let me make this as simple as possible – if you're not willing to leave behind what's most important to you, then you cannot be my disciple.

'You are salt. And salt is good. But if it loses its saltiness – the thing that makes it special and distinct – then it's no good for anything and just gets chucked in the bin.'

1, 2, 3, 4, 5, 6, 7.
Count the cost. Count the cost.
Count the cost in the kingdom of heaven.

What does it cost to follow Jesus?

It costs nothing at all – but it costs everything we've got.

How can that be?

Because nothing good happens in this world without sacrifice.

I'll say it again. Nothing good happens in this world without sacrifice. Nothing good happens without one person giving up something for someone else.

That's what Jesus did for us when he died on the cross.

And if we're going to follow him – live as he lived and see it through to the end – then we are going to find ourselves giving up things too. Even the most precious things we've got.

1, 2, 3, 4, 5, 6, 7.
Count the cost. Count the cost.
Count the cost in the kingdom of heaven.

That's the truth. That's the bottom line. That's what the journey is all about.

He who has ears, let him hear.

A Maths Problem

(Luke 15:1–2, 8–10)

**Telling tips: When you get to the 'counting' bits, ask your group to
count the numbers out on their fingers (or their toes!). You might
want to practice this ahead of time to get the rhythm right (or the
numbers right, depending on the mathematical ability of your
crowd!)**

Jesus was talking with the tax collectors and their friends. But the
Pharisees and their friends (who always seemed to be eavesdropping)
were listening as well.

'Look at that!' they muttered. 'He says he's a religious man, but
he spends all his time with sinners!'

So Jesus turned to the Pharisees and said, 'I've got a maths
problem for you. Add, subtract, multiply, divide. Use your fingers,
use your toes if you like. Here's the problem: "What number makes
an angel smile?"'

The Pharisees groaned. They hated maths – and those word
problems in particular. So while they were undoing their sandals,
Jesus told them a story.

Once there was a woman who had ten coins. And each coin was
worth a day's wage. One afternoon, she went to count her coins.
And suddenly, she had a maths problem too!

One, two, three.
Four, five, six.
Seven, eight, nine and ten.

That's how many there were supposed to be. But somehow, someone had done some subtracting. And now there were only nine!

Desperate for a solution, the woman tackled the problem at once. She lit a lamp. She swept the floor. She lost track of how much time it took. Inch by inch. Metre by metre. Cubit by cubit. The woman looked carefully into every crack and crevice. And finally, she found it!

Her deficit diminished. Her budget balanced. The woman counted her coins again.

One, two, three.
Four, five, six.
Seven, eight, nine and TEN!

And then she smiled. For that one last coin had made all the difference.

What number makes an angel smile? The answer is the same.

One.

Just one.

Each one.

Every one.

One missing soul swept out of the darkness and into the light. One lost sinner found. Do the maths. Add, subtract, multiply, divide. Use your fingers, use your toes if you like. You'll see that it all adds up.

The Other Prodigal

(Luke 15:25–32)

Telling tips: This is best read by one person. But it might be helpful to have someone else read the father's part.

The older brother became angry and refused to go in. So his father went out and pleaded with him. But he answered his father...

I can't go in. I just can't go in. I know you love him. I can see that you've forgiven him. But I can't forget the look on your face the day he left.

You were gutted. Devastated. Destroyed. You couldn't eat or sleep for weeks. Surely you remember.

And it wasn't easy for me either. There were jobs that needed to be done. Responsibilities he'd accepted that had to fall to someone else – me! To be honest, I felt abandoned too.

And yes, I can see that you're happy now. Just happy to see him again. To talk with him. I understand that. I really do. But how long will it last? That's what I want to know. Surely, you've asked yourself the same question?

He went away once. He took what he wanted. He left you for dead. So how long before he does it again? How many times will you let your heart be broken? That's what I want to know.

I mean, you can't really imagine that he's back for good. Things got hard for him out there – that's all. And he figured that things would be easier here. Oh, I know he said he'd gladly work as one of your servants. But he knows how well the servants are treated here. This is just the easy way out for him again. It's always the easy way out. So he swallows a little pride and comes back. Worst case scenario, you put him to work and he still gets three square meals a day and a warm place to sleep. Best case? Well, I think he's looking at the best case. Robes and rings and a feast the likes of which I've never seen.

I know. I know. I shouldn't bring it up. They're your robes and rings and caterers. Yours to do with as you please. It's just that... it's just that... if someone has to break your heart to get your attention, then your heart's going to be broken a lot.

'My son,' the father said, 'you are always with me, and everything I have is yours.'

I'm not saying I'm perfect. I'm not saying that for a minute. But I do try to do what's right. I really do. And I can't see what's wrong with that.

Loyalty. Commitment. Duty. OK, maybe those qualities aren't exciting. Maybe they're not compelling or sexy. But they are the qualities that hold things together. And they're qualities that I've learned from living with you!

I mean, what kind of state would the world be in if everyone acted like him? That's what I want to know. Taking what you want when you want it. Shirking your responsibilities. Running off at a moment's notice. Living for yourself, regardless of how your actions affect anyone else. That's what his life has been like. His and the millions of others who are just like him.

The problem is that it's the rest of us – the loyal, committed, duty-bound ones – who have to pick up the pieces, clear up the mess and pay the price when they're done.

And then, when they finally come running back home because the mess is too big, when they finally want some kind of help and support, we're not even allowed to criticize or complain. Oh no, because then WE would be in the wrong – uncaring, unsympathetic, unforgiving.

Well, who makes the effort to sympathize with us? That's what I want to know. Those of us who play by the rules and at least try to do what's right. Who takes the time to see things our way? To walk in our shoes?

No one. That's who. We just get called names. Legalists. Moralists. Conformists. Prudes.

'My son,' the father said, 'you are always with me, and everything I have is yours.'

I mean, what's so wrong with trying to do what's right and suggesting that if a few more people tried a bit harder, there might be less mess to clean up in the first place? What's so bad about encouraging people to take a little more responsibility for themselves?

I know. I know. I know. No one's perfect. Life's not like that. And I'm not always responsible either. Of course, we all need to be forgiven at one time or other. But some people – people like him – just seem to go out of their way to make a habit of it! As if the failing and the forgiving provides some kind of assurance – again and again and again – that they will be loved no matter what they do.

Maybe you don't mind. But I find it tiring. And frustrating. Living always with that uncertainty.

It reminds me of summer camp. That's what it does. There were these boys – popular boys. The ones who were good at sports and getting the girls. Well, year after year, these boys would mess up. They'd break the rules and get into all kinds of trouble. But then, the last night, around the campfire, they'd come forward in a flood of tears and say how sorry they were and how they were going to change and how things would be different. And they would cry and the camp counsellors would cry and the girls would cry.

But I didn't. I couldn't. And I could never figure out why no one seemed to remember that the same thing had happened the year before. And the year before that.

Were they just a bunch of dumb suckers, falling for the same old trick, year after year? Or was I the sucker? Because the other thing I could never figure out was why the same camp counsellors who got all choked up about those kids never had more than two words for the likes of us who kept the rules and didn't cause any trouble and memorized our verses without complaint. There were no tears for us. Not much attention of any kind, as I recall.

And so I have to ask. Have to ask again. What does it take – what does it take to get their attention? What does it take to get yours? Are you like the girl who ignores the guy who's kind to her because she finds the prospect of reforming the bad boy more appealing? Is that what this is all about? Because if it is, I feel duty-bound to remind you that she often ends up hurt and abused and pregnant.

And the nice guy? The nice guy just gets ignored.

The problem is that there's a world full of us. We're married to alcoholics and related to druggies. Our brothers-in-law are adulterers, our uncles are gamblers. Our mothers pop pills and our sisters abandon their kids.

So we mop up the puke and change the extra nappies and visit the hospitals and pay for the rehab and cancel the debts and put up with so much crap.

And what do we get in return? We get taken for granted most of the time. Or condemned – if we should so much as suggest that they should get their act together.

But do you know what we really want? All we really want is for someone to pay us a little bit of attention too.

'My son,' the father said, 'you are always with me, and everything I have is yours.'

He'd said that before. A couple times, I think. And at first, it sounded like condemnation.

'Stop your moaning. Don't complain. You have everything you need.'

But maybe it sounded that way because that's what I was expecting to hear.

Because when he said it the third time, it didn't sound as if he was criticizing me at all. It sounded more like a welcome. It sounded more like – I don't know – an invitation?

All right, it wasn't a feast he was offering. But then, I didn't need a feast. I hadn't been sharing scraps with sows, had I? I'd been eating well all along. And as for rings and robes, I had them too.

What I needed was... well, what I needed was him, I guess. Or at least the assurance that he understood.

But then I realized that's what he'd been giving me.

'You are always with me,' he'd said. 'I do pay attention to you. I do recognize and regard you. You're not alone. Not alone in your obedience, your faithfulness, or even in your frustration with a world that is not as it was meant to be. Not alone when you try to fix what's wrong or hang in there with someone. Not alone when you hold things together.

'Everything I have is yours,' he'd said. 'My goodness so you can be good. My faithfulness so you can be faithful. My patience so you can be patient. My strength so you can endure. You can't do any of that without me.'

And then there was that last thing. The thing that annoyed me when I first heard it, but that finally made sense in the end.

'We had to celebrate and be glad, because this brother of yours was dead and is alive again; he was lost and is found.'

It was the word 'dead' that did it. That finally changed my mind. How had my brother become a prodigal? By treating my dad as if he was dead. So if I did the same thing to my brother, if I left him in the grave when I could welcome him back to life, would that not make me a kind of prodigal too?

'All right,' I said. 'I'll do it.' And with the noise of the feast ringing in my ears, I swallowed my pride, like my brother had swallowed his. And I went in and sat down at my father's table.

Kids and Camels and the
Kingdom of God

(Luke 18)

**Telling tips: There are two motions that are at the heart of this
reading – welcoming (arms open wide, ready to receive) and pushing
away (hands out in front, pushing away). Lead your group in doing
those two motions whenever they appear in the text. The alternative
ending makes the reading a bit more specific and may not work in
every situation, but I have included it in case it works for you.**

When the women came to Jesus with their children, the disciples
pushed them away. But Jesus opened wide his arms and said,
'Don't keep the kids away from me. The kingdom of heaven
belongs to them. They're little and powerless, dependent and small.
And you need to be like them to find your way in!'

But when the ruler came to Jesus, with his goodness and his goods,
the disciples welcomed him with open arms. 'If this man can't be
saved,' they said, 'then who can?'

Jesus welcomed the man as well. But this is what he said:
'The only goodness there is, is God's. And as for your goods – give
them to the poor!'

So the man walked sadly away.

Jesus was sad as well. So he turned to his friends and said, 'The
rich own many things. But not the kingdom of God. It does not
belong to them. They are big and powerful, strong and

independent. And, like a camel shoved through the eye of a needle, they find it hard to let go of enough hump and hoof to squeeze in!

God's values are different from ours. That's all Jesus was trying to say. He welcomes those we push away. And those we welcome, he welcomes too. (They just can't push their way in!)

It sounds difficult. It sounds complicated. But it's simple really.

It's all about kids and camels and the kingdom of God.

(Alternative ending – pick up after '… hump and hoof to squeeze in!')

So when the rich man came to our church, we welcomed him with open arms. We gave him a cup of coffee and a comfy seat in a state-of-the-art sanctuary.

And when the children came, we welcomed them as well. We let them stay in the sanctuary (for the first thirty minutes). Then we sent them to the corner of the fellowship hall (which, admittedly, could use a coat of paint), with Mrs Robertson, who has served the Sunday School faithfully for ages (on a fifty-pound-per-year budget).

And that's when Jesus came to our church too. 'This is not hard,' he said. 'I'll go through it slowly if you like, because so much depends on you getting this.' And he told us again about kids and camels and the kingdom of God.

Another Maths Problem

(Luke 18:18–27)

Telling tips: This one's just for you to tell on your own. Have fun with it!

A disciple is a learner, a pupil, a student – someone who goes to school. So when the rich man asked his question – 'Good teacher, what must I do to inherit eternal life?' – Jesus' disciples thought it was time for RE.

Jesus knew different however. He was the teacher after all. And he could see, quite clearly, that the rich man's question was all about Maths.

'You know the commandments,' said Jesus.

'Don't murder;

'Don't commit adultery;

'Don't steal;

'Don't lie;

'Don't cheat;

'Honour your father and your mother.'

And like a man punching numbers into a calculator, or stacking up coins, or counting on his fingers, the rich man nodded, one by one.

'I have kept them all,' he said, 'ever since I was a boy!'

And that's when Jesus changed the subject – or at least the subject matter. 'You think the kingdom of God is all about addition,' he said. 'The problem is that no one can be as good as God – or add up enough good deeds to deserve eternal life.

'No, the kingdom is not about addition. It's about subtraction – taking away anything that stands between you and God and keeps you from devoting yourself to him. So if you want treasure in heaven, then you'll need to take away your earthly treasure and give it to the poor.'

The rich man was good at addition – in financial terms and in moral terms as well. But his calculator didn't even have a minus key, so he walked away sadly.

The disciples, meanwhile – the learners, the students – were trying to take all this in. Jesus could see the shocked looks on their faces. He could smell the smoke as their brains buzzed round a million miles a minute!

Riches are a blessing from God... That's what they were thinking. So a rich man should be closer to God than anyone!

'No,' said Jesus. 'You've got it all wrong. Riches make it harder for a man to get into the kingdom. His wealth becomes his god – it's what he depends on, treasures and serves. And it blocks his view of the true God in heaven.'

And that's when Jesus changed the subject again – to Zoology, and a bit of Home Economics.

'I tell you, it's easier for a camel to squeeze through the eye of a needle than for a rich man to get into God's kingdom.'

'Then how can anybody be saved?' cried the disciples.

'It's down to God,' said Jesus at last. 'It's always down to him – we must trust him to do what only he can do. None of us can save ourselves – no matter how many riches or good deeds we add up. But with God, anything and everything is possible!'

The Anatomy of Faith

(Luke 18:35–43)

Telling tips: You might want to just point to your ears, mouth, head and heart as you work your way through the reading. And then do it again, finishing off with your eyes.

He couldn't see. But there was nothing wrong with his ears.

'Who's there?' asked the blind beggar. 'What's going on? There's a crowd on its way, isn't there?'

'Jesus is coming,' said a beggar nearby. 'The crowd's with him.'

He couldn't see. But there was nothing wrong with his mouth.

'Jesus!' he shouted. 'Jesus, son of David, have mercy on me!'

And when there was no answer, he shouted even louder. 'Jesus!'

'Quiet!' said the people in the crowd. 'Stop your shouting, beggar!'

He couldn't see. But there was nothing wrong with his head.

He knew all about squeaky wheels. And grease.

So he shouted louder still, 'Jesus, son of David, have mercy on me!'

So Jesus stopped.

'What would you like me to do for you?' he asked.

He couldn't see. But there was nothing wrong with his heart.

'I don't want to be a blind beggar,' he said. 'I want to see.'

And Jesus said, 'So be it then. Your faith has made you whole.'

And now there was nothing wrong.
    Not with his ears.
    Not with his mouth.
    Not with his head.
    Not with his heart.
    And not with his eyes either.
    Not any more!

The Ballad of a Little Man

(Luke 19:1–10)

Telling tips: You might like to find volunteers to play Abraham and Nathaniel, and get them to react accordingly. You could even get someone small to play Zacchaeus. A chair, a pew, or a very tall deacon might make a good sycamore tree. Just check your liability insurance first!

Abraham was the town butcher.
He stood tall. He was honest and kind.
He sold chicken and cow.
The folks loved it – and how!
(And he never touched fried bacon rind!)

But Zacchaeus was a very little man,
And a very little man was he.
He was hated and feared.
No one wanted him near.
He was Jericho's taxman, you see!

Nathaniel was the town baker.
A big man, with five strapping sons.
All Jericho slobbered
And globbered and drooled
At the smell of his freshly baked buns.

But Zacchaeus was a very little man,
And a very little man was he.
For a few pennies more
He'd cheat you for sure
He'd do anything to increase his fee.

Now the word went around
Old Jericho Town
That Jesus was coming for tea.
'Twas an honour, a treat
For this teacher to eat
At one's house – so they lined up to see.

'Come eat with me!'
Tall Abraham said.
'We'll have drumsticks and lamb chops and beef!'
But Jesus just smiled
And passed on through the crowd,
Leaving Abraham stricken with grief.

'To my house he'll come,'
Nathaniel explained
To those standing 'round, with a boast.
But when he was asked
Jesus wandered right past.
Nate's mood turned as black as burnt toast.

Many others came next.
I suppose that you've guessed –
Jesus said 'no' to each of them too.
In fact, he said 'nay'
To all good folk that day,
And shaded his eyes for a view.

Zacchaeus, meanwhile,
With a chimpanzee's style,
Had climbed up a sycamore tree.
He was just curious
But the crowd might get furious
If they saw him. So he hid there safely!

Jesus looked down,
Quite close to the ground,
And failed there to find his prey.
A rustle. A cry.
So Jesus looked high.
The branches were starting to sway.

'So that's where you're hiding,
You very little man.
I'm hungry, and that's why I say:
Put your feet on the ground.
ZACCHAEUS, COME DOWN!
I'm eating at your house today.'

Zacchaeus was shocked.
And you could have knocked
The crowd over with a feather. And so,
Honoured and humbled,
He climbed down then stumbled
Homeward, with Jesus in tow.

The crowd muttered and moaned.
'A sinner!' they groaned.
'A scoundrel, a swindler, a swine!
It's a scandal, a curse.
It couldn't be worse!
Jesus sharing his bread and his wine.'

They talked all through tea.
What they said, no one knows.
No keyhole to hear or peep through.
But when they came out,
Jesus said, with a shout,
'Zacchaeus has now changed his view!'

'He's different, he's sorry.
He's forgiven. He's saved.
He's brand-spanking, fresh-smelling new.
He's still rather small.
But his heart's ten feet tall.
And now he will prove it to you.'

'To those that I've cheated,'
Said Zac with a smile,
'I'll pay back times two – no, times four!
And I've emptied my coffers.
I've got some great offers
For anyone out there who's poor.'

The people applauded.
They couldn't believe it.
'He's gentle and kind as a dove!'
Jesus said, with a grin.
'See, there's no one whose sin
Takes him out of the reach of my love.'

A Death Rewound

(Luke 24:1–12, Matthew 28:8–10, John 20:14–18)

Telling tips: Here's another one just to tell on your own.

Mary Magdalene remembered.

How could she ever forget? The drawn face. The sunken eyes. The final breath. The moment he died. Then the thunder and the lightning and the shaking of the ground. The shaking of her shoulders and his mother's shoulders too as their tears mixed with the rain.

There was no rain now. But there were tears. Tears and dew and early morning mist, as she made her way slowly to the tomb. Suddenly, the ground began to shake, and she feared for a moment that it was happening all over again. And in a way – in a backwards kind of way – it was!

There was thunder and there was lightning, and the soldiers were terrified as they had been three days before. Then the tomb split open – wide open like the curtain in the temple – and all in a great rush, an angel told Mary and her friends that Jesus was alive. His face was shining bright and he had so much more to say. And perhaps the other women listened, but Mary Magdalene just looked. For there was only one face she wanted to see. And when at last she did see it, that other picture was erased for ever. This face was not drawn; it sported a wide and knowing smile. These eyes were not sunken; they burned bright with life and promise. And the breath he took to speak finished not with a goodbye, but with a warm and glad hello.

Jesus was alive! And even though he went away again, Mary remembered. Mary Magdalene remembered. How could she ever forget?

Three Men and a Fig Tree

(*John 1:43–51*)

Telling tips: You could either divide your group into four sections,
then on the 'Jesus, Nathanael, Philip and the fig tree' line, group
one could be Jesus (arms open wide), group two could be Nathanael
(arms crossed and suspicious look on face), group three could be
Philip (waving as if to say, 'Come on!') and group four could be
the fig tree (arms as branches – either waving or fixed in some
contorted manner!). Or divide the group into four sections and get
them to take it in turns to be the fig tree. It's a bit more fun and
keeps them focused.

Jesus said to Philip, 'Follow me!'
Jesus, Nathanael, Philip and the fig tree.
So Philip found his friend, sitting under a tree.

'We've found him, Nathanael! The one we've been waiting for!'
Jesus, Nathanael, Philip and the fig tree.
'The messiah, promised by Moses and the prophets!'

'His name is Jesus – Jesus of Nazareth.'
Jesus, Nathanael, Philip and the fig tree.
Nathanael scoffed. He was a bit of a snob.

'Nothing good has ever come from Nazareth!'
Jesus, Nathanael, Philip and the fig tree.
'You'll see!' said Philip. 'Just come and see!'

So they left the fig tree and went to find Jesus.
Jesus, Nathanael, Philip and the fig tree.
And when Jesus saw them coming, he opened his arms.

'Nathanael!' he said. 'Nathanael, I know you!'
Jesus, Nathanael, Philip and the fig tree.
'You speak your mind. You mean what you say.'

'And when you see the truth, you want to embrace it.
Jesus, Nathanael, Philip and the fig tree.
'A true Israelite – with nothing false about you.'

Nathanael was puzzled. 'But how do you know me?'
Jesus, Nathanael, Philip and the fig tree.
'We've never met. Not that I can recall.'

'I saw you,' said Jesus. 'Underneath the fig tree.'
Jesus, Nathanael, Philip and the fig tree.
'I saw you while Philip was on his way.'

Nathanael was amazed – amazed and astounded.
Jesus, Nathanael, Philip and the fig tree.
'Then you must be the messiah – the Son of God!'

'Surprised?' said Jesus. 'We've only just started.'
Jesus, Nathanael, Philip and the fig tree.
'You'll see angels in heaven by the time we're done.'

So Nathanael followed Jesus, just like Philip.
Jesus, Nathanael, Philip and the fig tree.
And off they went. What adventures they had!
Jesus, Nathanael, Philip and the fig tree.

Make the Wind Blow

(Acts 2)

Telling tips: You need to teach the chorus at the beginning. I have included the actions in the text.

Jesus' friends were watching and praying.
Praying for the present that he had promised.
Praying together in the city of Jerusalem.
Praying on the Feast of Pentecost.

Jesus' friends were watching and praying
When all of a sudden, their prayers were answered.
They heard the roar of a rushing wind.
And tongues of fire licked their heads.

Make the wind blow. (Wave hands like the wind.)
Make the fire glow. (Make shape with hands like fire.)
Take the words from your lips (Pretend to touch God's lips.)
And put them on our lips (Touch own lips.)
And speak them out to the whole of the world. (Make shape of world.)

Jesus' friends were watching and praying
When the Holy Spirit came upon them
Filled them, thrilled them and spilled right out of them
With words they did not know.

'What's going on?' asked the people of Jerusalem.
'What can this possibly mean?
These are plain Galileans, ordinary folk,
Speaking words they could never have learned.'

Make the wind blow.
Make the fire glow.
Take the words from your lips
And put them on our lips
And speak them out to the whole of the world.

'We come from the north, the south, and the east.
We come from all over the world!
Yet we all understand the things that they say
As they tell out the wonders of God.'

But some of the crowd were not so impressed.
Some even said they were drunk!
And that's when Peter, Jesus' friend,
Stood up and put them right.

Make the wind blow.
Make the fire glow.
Take the words from your lips
And put them on our lips
And speak them out to the whole of the world.

'Filled with wine?' he said. 'Not likely!
But we're filled with something else!
Filled with God's own Holy Spirit –
The power the prophets promised.'

'And how did this happen?' asked Peter.
I'll tell you plain and true.
This is the gift of Jesus, the messiah,
Whom you killed just six weeks ago!'

Make the wind blow.
Make the fire glow.
Take the words from your lips
And put them on our lips
And speak them out to the whole of the world.

The people were sorry, sad and ashamed.
And they cried, 'What can we do?'
'Repent and be baptized,' said Peter plainly.
And this gift will come to you!'

So the people repented, the people were baptized.
Three thousand people – or so!
And the word spread from there to the rest of Judea
And on to the rest of the world!

Make the wind blow.
Make the fire glow.
Take the words from your lips
And put them on our lips
And speak them out to the whole of the world.

A Visit to Lystra

(Acts 14:8–18)

**Telling tips: This is one of those stories where you explain the story
before you actually tell it! Say that it's about Paul and Barnabas and
their first visit to Lystra. They see a lame man, and at that point we
all grab our legs and say, 'OW!' The lame man is healed, so we all say
'WOW!' The people in the town think Paul and Barnabas are gods,
so we all act like ancient Greek gods, throw thunderbolts and shout,
'KAPOW!' The people bring them offerings, so we hold our fingers
against our temples like horns and everyone will pretend to be a
COW. Paul and Barnabas are horrified by this behaviour. They are
not gods, they explain. We join them by stamping our feet and
demanding that the people take the gifts away right NOW! And then,
as Paul and Barnabas seize the opportunity to talk about their faith,
we will join them as they point their audience to the True God, unto
whom they should BOW. The repetition in each verse is there both
to build some tension (as you say it a bit louder each time) and to
give the crowd the chance to really get into the participation.**

Paul and Barnabas were preaching in Lystra.
Paul and Barnabas were preaching in Lystra.
Paul and Barnabas were preaching in Lystra.
When they spotted a lame man. (OW!)
When they spotted a lame man. (OW!)
When they spotted a lame man. (OW!)

'You can be healed!' said Paul to the lame man.
'You can be healed!' said Paul to the lame man.
'You can be healed!' said Paul to the lame man.
And the man jumped up and walked. (WOW!)
And the man jumped up and walked. (WOW!)
And the man jumped up and walked. (WOW!)

'These men must be gods!' cried the people of Lystra.
'These men must be gods!' cried the people of Lystra.
'These men must be gods!' cried the people of Lystra.
Gods like Hermes and Zeus. (KAPOW!)
Gods like Hermes and Zeus. (KAPOW!)
Gods like Hermes and Zeus. (KAPOW!)

So they brought them gifts and sacrifices.
So they brought them gifts and sacrifices.
So they brought them gifts and sacrifices.
Fancy wreaths and a COW.
Fancy wreaths and a COW.
Fancy wreaths and a COW.

'We are not gods!' cried Paul and Barnabas.
'We are not gods!' cried Paul and Barnabas.
'We are not gods!' cried Paul and Barnabas.
Take these away right NOW!
Take these away right NOW!
Take these away right NOW!

'We worship the God who made heaven and earth.'
'We worship the God who made heaven and earth.'
'We worship the God who made heaven and earth.'

'Unto him you should BOW.'
'Unto him you should BOW.'
'Unto him you should BOW.'

OW, WOW, KAPOW, COW,
NOW unto him you should BOW.

Walk and Pray and Listen

Acts 16:6–10

Telling tips: It's pretty obvious how to tell this one. And it's incredibly repetitive – but that's the point! Sometimes we just have to be patient and keep at it. So get your group to make a walking motion, a praying motion and then to put their hands to their ears in a listening motion.

Paul and Silas and Timothy
Walked and prayed and listened.
They were looking for a place to talk about Jesus,
So they walked and prayed and listened.

They came to the borders of the province of Asia
As they walked and prayed and listened.
But the Spirit told them to move along
So they walked and prayed and listened.

Day after day, week after week,
They walked and prayed and listened.
Up hill and down hill and across vast plains
They walked and prayed and listened.

They came to the borders of the province of Mysia
As they walked and prayed and listened.
But the spirit of Jesus sent them on
So they walked and prayed and listened.

Week after week, month after month
They walked and prayed and listened.
For 200, 300, 400 miles
They walked and prayed and listened!

Then they came to the sea – to the port of Troas
As they walked and prayed and listened.
And Paul had a dream – a dream of a man
As they walked and prayed and listened.

'Come, talk to us,' the dream man said.
'As you walk and pray and listen.
'Across the sea to Macedonia.
'Come walk, I pray, and we'll listen.'

So Paul and Silas and Timothy
Walked and prayed and listened
Across the sea to Macedonia
They walked and prayed and listened.

And they talked to the people
And the people believed;
Churches were planted,
The Good News received!

But it wouldn't have happened
If they'd just stopped at home
Or got tired and quit
Or asked a consultant
Or taken a poll
Or made a grand plan
Or just done what they wanted.
No it only happened, only happened at all
Because Paul and Silas and Timothy
Walked and prayed and listened.

A Prison in Philippi

(Acts 16:16–34)

Telling tips: Divide your group into three. Give each group a line of the chorus and encourage them to pull their hands apart as if their chains have been broken.

> *Loose the bonds,*
> *Break the chains,*
> *Set the prisoner free.*

The girl was enslaved, imprisoned, trapped. Possessed by a demon and by her human masters as well, who used the powers the demon gave her to make themselves a fortune. 'She'll tell your future! Interpret your dreams. Put your money on the table!' they shouted to the crowds in Philippi.

> *Loose the bonds,*
> *Break the chains,*
> *Set the prisoner free.*

Then Paul and Silas came to Philippi to talk about Jesus. And when she saw them, the slave girl shouted, 'These men are the servants of the Most High God.'

Her words were true, but Paul was worried – worried at the poor girl's situation and worried as well that the crowd would confuse his message with the power of the demon.

So Paul told the demon, 'In the name of Jesus,

Loose the bonds,
Break the chains,
Set the prisoner free.

And the demon came out of the girl!

That should have been that – the end of the story. But the girl had masters, remember? And the men who had made a fortune from her saw their business plan wrecked in a second. Their share prices slipping. Their stocks in free fall. They knew that they had to blame someone, so they got the authorities to arrest Paul and Silas and beat them and throw them in prison. And the men who had set the slave girl free were now trapped and imprisoned themselves!

Loose the bonds,
Break the chains,
Set the prisoner free.

Paul was enslaved, imprisoned, trapped and so was Silas his friend. Their cell door locked. Their feet in stocks. They were stuck in a foreign jail. They might have complained. They might have cursed. They might have rung their solicitor. But instead, they sang, they sang and prayed, prayed and sang praises to God.

Loose the bonds,
Break the chains,
Set the prisoner free.

Shaking and quaking and making such noise, an earthquake broke into their song.

Shaking and quaking and breaking the locks, an earthquake broke open their cell.

Shaking and quaking and taking his sword, the jailer went to kill himself, for the law was clear: if the prisoners escaped, he would have to die in their place.

Loose the bonds,
Break the chains,
Set the prisoner free.

Now the jailer was enslaved, imprisoned, trapped. There was no way out but death. But then Paul cried, 'Don't hurt yourself! Every one of us is still here.'

Shaking and quaking and taking a torch, the jailer went round to see. Paul's word were true. Not one had escaped. And the jailer fell to his knees.

Loose the bonds,
Break the chains,
Set the prisoner free.

'I've heard you sing, I've heard you pray, I've seen the saving power of your God. So tell me,' he said to Paul and Silas, 'what must I do to be saved?'

So Paul and Silas told him about Jesus, told all of his family too. And after he'd washed them and dressed their wounds the jailer was washed and made new. Washed in baptism. Washed clean of his sins. And all of his family too. Washed and set free by the men he'd imprisoned. Washed and set free and made new.

Loose the bonds,
Break the chains,
Set the prisoner free.

Location! Location! Location!

(Hebrews 3:1–11)

Telling tips: This is one where you should probably read the Bible text first. The participation is really simple. Divide your group into three and then get each group to shout 'Location!', getting a little bit louder each time.

Location! Location! Location!

Let's be honest here, shall we? The Israel House was adequate at the time. It was sturdy. It was functional. It was, after all, God, himself, who built it. But it was only a starter home. The first step on the property ladder that leads to our heavenly mansion. And Moses was a faithful servant in that house. He didn't own it. He didn't even rent. He was more like a live-in handyman. Laying down the law, and the tiles on the kitchen floor. Taking up our cause to God with the old lino in the hall. Paving the way to the promised land and the path to the garden shed. He was Laurence Llewelyn-Bowen with beard and sandals. Charlie Dimmock with a great big pair of stone tablets. His job was to fix the place up. Get it ready to sell. So all of us could move on.

Location! Location! Location!

Now we live in the Jesus house. And you've got to admit – it's a much better proposition, all round. Bigger rooms, so more of us can squeeze in. More doors to enter. More windows, more light. And not so many rules. We can tidy up on Saturday if we like. And make whatever we want in the kitchen. It's a gracious, spacious place to live. And that's because Jesus doesn't just work here. He's not just a handyman. He owns the place.

Oh, the jobs are much the same. Revealing God's will and his plans for the place. Cementing our relationship with him and the cracks that come between us. And installing the odd skylight so we can look to heaven as well. But because the house is his, he has far more invested in it than any workman could ever have. Just think what it cost him in the first place.

Location! Location! Location!

So let's live in the Jesus house. Let's trust in the one who owns it and follow his household rules. And let's not make the mistake they made in the Israel house. They rebelled against the builder – remember? They disbelieved, they disobeyed, they gave up and tried to tear the place down. And what happened? They ended up with negative equity on a rundown property in an unfashionable desert district, sandwiched between a camel factory and a neighbour with a rusting Sierra in his front garden. It took them forty years to sell that place. And I'd hate to see the same thing happen to us. Because we want to keep moving up that property ladder, don't we? And there's a mansion waiting for us. One that Jesus himself has prepared. So let's fix our eyes on him, the apostle and high priest we confess. And let's follow him up that ladder. Because it's all about...

Location! Location! Location!

Now That's What I Call Music!

(Hebrews 8)

Telling tips: It will be helpful to read Hebrews 8:1–7 before the reading. And then get the audience to do the 'Now that's what I call music!' bit.

Now that's what I call music!

Let's be honest here, shall we? 'Moses and the Twelve Tribes' was a great band. Memorable tunes. Solid vocals. First-class musicians. And the gigs they played at The Tabernacle deserve their place in history.

But when it comes down to it, Moses and the Twelve Tribes was really just a tribute band. The Rolling Clones, The Illegal Eagles, The Karaoke Covenant, if you like. Nothing more than a copy of a better band, on a bigger stage, with a belting lead singer – the true Godfather of Soul.

And that's the problem with tribute bands. The lyrics have to be memorized. The posturing imitated. The guitar solos practiced to perfection. And the costumes and hair recreated exactly. Everything according to pattern – from the outside in. Which is fine as far as it goes. Until the real band comes to town.

Now that's what I call music!

They know the words. They wrote them. They've been singing them for years. The performance is like second nature. The hair and the clothes are their own. They fit them. And the solos spring to the fingers from somewhere deep inside.

> **After that time, declares the Lord, I will put my laws in their minds and write them on their hearts. I will be their God, and they will be my people. No longer will a man teach his neighbour, or a man his brother, saying, 'Know the Lord,' because they will all know me.**

Or to borrow a lyric: 'Jesus put this song into our hearts.'

Now that's what I call music!

A Dying Dream

(Hebrews 9, Revelation 15)

**Telling tips: You might want to read parts of Hebrews 9 before
sharing this reading. I would suggest either verses 1–14 (which set
up the context nicely), or if that seems too long, just verses 11–14.**

He slipped into a stupor, a daze, a dream. And, suddenly, he was no
longer suspended in the air. He was walking slowly through the
tent. The light from the lampstand sent his shadow trembling
across the walls. He bumped into a table and picked some bread up
off a plate. This is my body, he thought.

And then he saw the curtain and the altar and heard the voices
of the beasts. The bleating of goats. The calves crying for their
mothers. Millions upon millions of them. And the knives raised
and the throats slit and the blood. The blood everywhere, over
everything. The blood upon the altar. This is my blood, he
thought.

And now the knife was in his hand. He was the High Priest
Aaron. He was Abraham on the mountain. And he was the goat
bleating for mercy as well. The calf crying for its mother. And Isaac
asking his father, 'Why?'

So he cried for his mother, 'Take care of her, John!'

And he cried to his father, 'Why? Why have you forsaken me?'

And he drew the knife across his wrists and feet and across his
head and plunged it into his side. And the blood poured out.
Everywhere, over everything. Everywhere, over everyone. The
blood upon the altar. And that's when the curtain opened. Not

drawn open. Not pulled open. But torn open. Curtain rails wrecked. Fabric on the floor. Never to be shut again.

Then he walked through the place where the curtain had been, into the place beyond. And like Isaac skipping down the mountain, that's where he found the answer to his question. For there was his Father. All that smelled and felt and tasted of him. The fresh manna of his provision. The chiselled words of his will. The budding staff of his beauty and power. And the soft beaten gold at the seat of his mercy.

Above that seat the angels sang. But they did not sing alone. For there were other voices too. The voices of everyone who had slipped into that place behind him. Behind him and because of him. Through the blood, across the rags of the curtain and into the presence of the Father. Millions upon millions of them. Swelling the place with their bodies and with their song. Not the bleating of goats, nor the cry of calves, but the grateful praise of the forgiven, mixing with the incense and rising to the Father.

Great and marvellous are your deeds, Lord God Almighty. Just and true are your ways, King of the ages. Who will not fear you, O Lord, and bring glory to your name? For you alone are holy. All nations will come and worship before you. For your righteous acts have been revealed.

'It is finished,' he said, with the song ringing in his ears. 'It is finished.' And the dream faded. And the stupor cleared. And he closed his eyes and died.

Clouds and Crowds
and Witnesses

(Hebrews 11, 12)

Telling tips: I know that, strictly speaking, we're the ones who need to be looking at 'the cloud of witnesses' as our inspiration and example, as opposed to the other way round. But I thought it would be nice to push the racing imagery and have it both ways! The cheering is the key participation device here. You could get everyone to do it together (either straight after the word 'cheering' or at the end of the first line). Or you could divide them into groups and work your way along to make the cheer louder – in a kind of 'wave' cheer.

They're cheering. Can you hear them?
Like a cloud, they surround us.
The ones who've run the race before.

Abel and Enoch,
Noah and Abraham,
Isaac and Jacob and Joseph and Moses

Look at them training.
Take note of their technique.
They'll teach us how to run the race.

They're cheering. Can you hear them?
Like a cloud, they surround us.
The ones who've run the race before.

Rahab and Gideon,
Barak and Samson,
Jephthah and David and Samuel and the prophets

Throw off everything that holds you back.
Like Noah threw off his doubt,
Like Abraham threw off his homeland,
Like Enoch threw off the weight of the world and went to walk
    with God.

Throw off whatever is wrong as well – whatever tempts and tangles
    and trips you up.
Like Rahab threw off her idols,
Like Jacob threw off his deceit,
Like Moses threw off the pleasures of sin and chose the plight of
    his people.

Then run with perseverance. Run the whole course and never give up.
Like Joseph waiting for his dreams to come true,
Like Samuel's search for a king,
Like Gideon watching his army weaken to the point he could
    claim God's victory.

They're cheering. Can you hear them?
Like a cloud, they surround us.
The ones who've run the race before.

And out in front, out in front of us all
Is the one on whom we fix our eyes.
He's setting the pace. He's leading the race.
The author and perfecter of our faith.

He hurdles the shame,
He fights through the pain.
It looks as if the race will be lost.
But in spite of his foes
He endures, wins, then throws
His arms wide in the shape of a cross.

So let's run the race.
Run and not grow weary.
Run for the prize that's set before us.

And when we get run down,
Let's look and let's listen.
For we don't run this race alone.

They're cheering. Can you hear them?
Like a cloud, they surround us.
The ones who've run the race before.

A Choosy People

(1 Peter 2:9–10)

Telling tips: Yet another story for two tellers. As in the others like this the Bible quotes should be said quite seriously. But the passages in between have quite a different feel!

> **But you are a chosen people, a royal priesthood, a holy nation, a people belonging to God, that you may declare the praises of him who called you out of darkness into his wonderful light.**

When we first moved to town, we had a pretty clear idea of the kind of church we were looking for.

The worship had to be right, for a start.

> **But you are a chosen people, a royal priesthood, a holy nation, a people belonging to God.**

Post-Kendrick. Pre-Redman. A touch of Taizé. That's what we had in mind. And we thought we'd found it. But when the organist at the first church we joined played the chorus of 'Shine, Jesus, shine' while the offering was being collected, we knew there and then that the Lord was telling us to leave.

> **That you may declare the praises of him who called you out of darkness into his wonderful light.**

The next church was better. Yes, they seemed to love God and love one another. But they weren't really in touch with the Spirit. They weren't 'moving on'. If you know what I mean.

But you are a holy nation, a royal priesthood.

So we tried a church on the other side of town. Sadly, the pastor was entirely too legalistic. He wouldn't let women pray!

A holy nation, a people belonging to God.

While the vicar at the next place was entirely too loose. He wanted women priests!

That you may declare the praises of him

So God called us on. What could we do?

Who called you out of darkness into his wonderful light.

But everywhere we went it was the same story.

But you are a chosen people,

The paintwork was too bright.

A royal priesthood,

The drums were too loud.

A holy nation,

The incense made me sneeze.

A people belonging to God.

The woman sitting next to me had a funny nose.

That you may declare the praises of him who called you out of darkness into his wonderful light.

I think the church is like a supermarket! If you don't like the quality of the produce at Tesco's, you can always pop down to Sainsbury's. Or ASDA. Or even the corner shop. Choice – that's the important thing. Keeping the customer satisfied. And I'm sure that's true of church as well.

But you are a chosen people.

Three Days of the Dragon

**Telling tips: I told this story in four parts at Spring Harvest's Good
Morning Big Top in 2002. I've divided it into those same parts for this
book and I've included telling tips at the start of each 'chapter'. You
might want to break it up that way as well, or just tell it in one go.**

Chapter One

**Telling tips: You can divide the audience into three groups: 'women',
'children' and 'men'. Before starting the story, show each group what
to do. The women can chat. The children can play (and sing 'la-la-la-
la-la'). And the men can laugh and wave pretend glasses and make
carousing noises! They then do that on cue in the story – altering
their actions to the described behaviour the second time around.**

Once upon a time, there was a river. It flowed through the middle of
a dry and mountainous land. And it flowed between two tribes – the
Tiana and the Aroman.

When the river flowed fast and full, both tribes drank from it
and watered their cattle and washed their clothes. Their women
chatted, their children played, and their men laughed and drank
and traded goods.

But when, one summer, the water flowed slow and shallow – and
when that summer stretched to a year and then two – the chatting
turned to argument, the playing turned to name-calling, and the
laughing and the trading turned to war.

Men on both sides died. Just a few at first – then more and many more. And that is when Tiana-Rom, chief of the Tiana tribe, came to his elders with an idea.

'The legends say there is a dragon who lives in the Far Mountains. A dragon that will come to the aid of any tribe that is willing to pay the price.'

'We don't need any help!' argued one of the elders. 'We are strong. We can do this ourselves!'

'It's a risk,' said another. 'And what if the legends are wrong? I say we stick to what we know and keep on fighting.'

'We need time to think,' said a third elder. 'We've never done it this way before.'

'And besides,' said the oldest elder of them all. 'You haven't yet told us what price this dragon demands.'

Tiana-Rom looked solemnly around the room. 'A life,' he whispered. 'The life of a brave young girl.' Then he nodded to a servant by the door, and into the room walked the chief's own daughter, Tiana-Mori.

'No!' cried the elders as one. 'Never!'

'But I have already agreed,' said Tiana-Mori. 'And I will go whether you permit me to or not. We do need help. We have run out of time. And each day more of our people die. This is a great risk, yes. But surely it is better to lose just one more life, than for all of us to perish.'

The elders looked at one another. This was indeed the bravest girl in the village. And that made their decision doubly hard. But their people needed water. The tribes were evenly matched. And the dragon would give them the advantage they required.

And so, sadly, they agreed.

Tiana-Mori left the very next morning. She walked for a day and a night and another day. And finally, at the foot of the tallest mountain, she came to the mouth of the dragon's cave. Bones were scattered everywhere. Tree branches rattled, bare and burned. And the dragon lay sleeping. His scales shimmered green and gold, and atop his head – like a cockerel's comb – ran a ridge of bright red horns. He was both the most frightening and the most beautiful creature that Tiana-Mori had ever seen.

For a second, just a second, Tiana-Mori thought about running. But at that very same second, the dragon stirred. He opened one green eye. He stared right at her. And then, to her amazement, the dragon spoke!

Chapter Two

Telling tips: For the second part, encourage the children to climb up on their parents' backs or shoulders and ride them like Tiana-mori rides the dragon. You could get a few people from the audience to model that for them on the stage. We had lots of fun (and a few calls to the local chiropractor).

'Is there something you want?' the dragon muttered. 'Something important enough to wake a dragon from his sleep?'

'There is,' said Tiana-Mori. 'I have come from the tribe of Tiana. I am the bravest girl in the village. And I am here to sacrifice myself so that you will help us defeat our enemy, the Aroman.'

'The bravest girl?' said the dragon, both eyes open now. 'Really? Well, why don't you climb onto my head, and we'll see about that.'

Tiana-Mori walked slowly towards the dragon. Past his sharp teeth and his shiny split tongue. Onto his paw and up his long foreleg. Over his mountain of a shoulder and finally up onto his head.

Was he playing with her? she wondered. Like a big cat, waiting for just the right moment to strike? Why didn't he just eat her and get it over with!

'Now sit down between the horns,' said the dragon. 'And hold on tight!'

And without another word, up the dragon flew – out of the mouth of the cave and high above the mountains, so quickly that Tiana-Mori could hardly catch her breath.

Up they flew, up towards the clouds – the dragon twisting and turning, and Tiana-Mori hanging on for dear life.

'Afraid yet, brave girl?' roared the dragon.

'Yes!' shouted Tiana-Mori, her eyes shut tight. 'But I will not let go, no matter how hard you try and shake me loose. For my people need me and I will do what I must do.'

'Very well, then,' the dragon replied. And he stopped his twisting and his turning and floated gently back towards the ground.

Tiana-Mori opened her eyes, relieved. But her relief did not last long.

For the dragon was not returning to his mountain cave. No, he was doing something far worse. There, ahead, lay her village. And there, beyond it, the dry river. The dragon was doing the most awful thing of all. Her mission unfinished, the dragon was taking her home!

They landed just outside the village, and as the tribe ran to meet them, Tiana-Mori pleaded with the dragon.

'Eat me now!' she cried. 'Spare my father and my friends from the sight of the thing you must do!'

'Eat you?' said the dragon. 'Wherever did you get that idea?'

'The legends,' answered Tiana-Mori.

'The legends?' snorted the dragon. 'The legends? Well, let me tell you this, young lady. I don't care what the legends say. There is more than one way to win the help of a dragon. And you have done so with your bravery and your selflessness. There is no doubt in my mind that you love your people and would do whatever it takes to save them. So go! Go and tell them that the dragon will come to their aid!'

Chapter Three

Telling tips: This is my favourite section, because we all get to play dragons! You can get everyone to take their jumpers or jackets or fleeces and wear them on their heads. (If you take the neck-hole

154

and jam it on your head like a hat, then the sleeves hang down beside your face and look like great big floppy ears!) Then get everyone to shake their heads about when the dragons play (leap, soar, turn, roar…) near the end of this section.

Tiana-Mori scrambled down from the dragon's head and ran to meet her father. She told him everything that had happened, and he hugged her and thanked her and gathered the elders together to make their war plans.

'Come, Dragon!' he said. 'Come meet with our council. It is good to have you on our side.'

'I will meet with you later,' the dragon shrugged. 'I have something more important to do right now.' And he turned to walk away.

'But, the legends…' said Tiana-Rom.

'The legends!' snorted the dragon. 'Don't talk to me about the legends.' And with a flap of his wings and a puff of smoke, he was gone.

'He's not what I expected, Father,' said Tiana-Mori.

'No,' grunted Tiana-Rom. 'Just as long as we can count on him. That's the important thing.' And they walked home, hand in hand.

As a reward for her bravery, Tiana-Mori was invited to the meeting as well. She sat in the corner of the hut. She listened carefully to the plans. She was fascinated by every detail. She was certain that her people would win. And when the meeting was over, she went to find the dragon and tell him everything that she had heard.

The dragon, however, was still not interested. Not interested at all. He was lying on his back, at the edge of the village. And the Tiana children were bouncing on his belly, and hanging off his tail, while their mothers watched and laughed.

'Dragon!' cried Tiana-Mori. 'You said you were on our side! You said you were loyal to us! Don't you care what the war plans are? Don't you know that you and you alone can strengthen the hearts of our people!'

The dragon picked the children, one by one, from his belly and gently set them down. Then he rolled over and looked straight into Tiana-Mori's eyes.

'There is more than one way to win the heart of a people,' he said. 'Listen to their laughter. And then go and ask your elders if they really want to turn that laughter into tears. For that is what their war will do.'

'I don't understand!' shouted Tiana-Mori. 'What about the legends?'

'The legends,' the dragon sighed. Then he picked up Tiana-Mori, and set her, once again, on his head. He tore off into the evening sky, blowing pinwheels of fire to the cheers of the children below. He flew straight for the ceiling of clouds. He burst straight through. And when he did, Tiana-Mori just stared and gasped.

The sun stood at one end of the sky, setting in a sea of blazing orange and pink. The moon stood high at the other end, like a ghost in the advancing blue of night. And between them, over a soft white floor of cloud, soared more dragons than Tiana-Mori could count.

There were giant purple ones, bigger than whales. Tiny red ones, smaller than hummingbirds. And every size between. Some had wings like bats. Some had wings like fairies. Some had no wings at all, but still somehow managed to fly.

They leaped.

They soared.

They turned.

They roared.

They shook their dragon heads

'What are they doing?' asked Tiana-Mori. 'Are they going to have a fight?'

'A fight?' snorted the dragon. 'Heavens, no! They're playing! It's what they do every night. I bet your legends don't tell you that!'

'But I thought dragons were...'

'Vicious? Fierce? Likely to gobble up brave little girls? Is that what you were going to say?' asked the dragon.

'Yes,' whispered Tiana-Mori. And then she fell silent.

'We were that way once,' the dragon admitted. 'But then, then we discovered this. This beauty. This joy. This play. This peace. And that is our only loyalty now.'

'But what about us?' asked Tiana-Mori. 'What about being loyal to us? You promised you would come! You promised you would help! Are you saying you no longer want to defeat our enemy?'

'I have come. And I will help,' the dragon grinned. 'And if all goes well, when I am finished the Aroman will no longer be your enemy. And perhaps then you will finally understand.'

Then he waved goodbye to the other dragons, dropped through the clouds and carried Tiana-Mori back to her home.

Chapter Four

Telling tips: In this section get everyone to stomp and breathe fire and shake the earth (beat feet on ground).

The next morning dawned drizzling and grey, and the dragon sat like an enormous dog and listened patiently to Tiana-Rom.

'The plan is quite simple,' he explained. 'Go before us. Blow fire, shake the earth. Terrify our enemy. Then be the bridge that we cross to crush them!'

Everything went well, at first. The dragon stomped out in front of the Tiana warriors, breathing fire and shaking the earth. And the Aroman army shook as well. But when the dragon reached the middle of the riverbed, he stopped and he stood between the two tribes. And he spoke.

'People of Tiana! People of Aroman! Once you lived in peace. You can live that way again! And I have come to show you how.'

'Peace?' cried Tiana-Rom. 'When we are so close to victory? Never!'

And in his rage, Tiana-Rom let one arrow fly – an arrow that struck the Aroman chief and killed him where he stood.

'See!' he shouted to the dragon. 'The legends were right! This is what you have come for – not for peace, but to help us defeat the enemy!'

And so pleased was Tiana-Rom with his shot that he did not see the arrow shot in return – the arrow that would surely have pierced his own heart, had someone not leaped in the way.

'Tiana-Mori!' cried the chief. But it was already too late. His only daughter lay dying in his arms.

'The legends! The legends!' roared the dragon. 'The sacrifice of a brave young girl. A dragon's aid. Now I will show you what the legends really mean!'

And as the arrows flew thick and fast, and as many more warriors fell, the dragon tore into the sky. High and higher he soared, till he was but a bright speck among the dark clouds. Then he dived straight towards the earth, faster than the driving rain – down, down, down, until he struck the riverbed with a mighty crash!

The force of the landing knocked the warriors from their feet. And when they rose, and when they looked, the dragon was gone. But the river was flowing fast and full!

Green and gold the water shimmered. And a voice called out from the deep.

'You must hurry. The time will soon be past. Come together to the river. Wash your dead in the water. And they will live.'

So that is what the two tribes did. Tiana-Rom went first, carrying Tiana-Mori. And the Aroman followed, with their fallen chief. They dragged the rest of the dead in as well. And there, in the river, the warriors of Tiana and the warriors of Aroman came back to life!

And that was not all. As they waded and splashed, as they shared their grief and their joy, the people of Tiana and Aroman looked into each other's faces for the first time in a long time. And they remembered. They remembered the chatting and the playing and the laughing and the days when the river was full. And so, something else came back to life as well. And the two tribes agreed to be friends, once again.

Washed and wet, they embraced one another, and so caught up were they in their reunion, that they did not notice the bridge – a ridge of bright red horns, like a cockerel's comb – that grew from one side of the river to the other.

That evening, as the tribes ate and drank and celebrated their peace, Tiana-Mori sat on the bridge and stared into the water.

'I'll miss you,' she said. 'And I'm sorry. I'm sorry that I did not trust you. But I understand now. I really do. There's more than one way to do everything. To win the help of a dragon. To win the heart of a people.'

'Yes,' rose a voice from the river. 'And there's more than one way to win a battle too.'

And then a shadow rose from the river as well – green and gold so that only Tiana-Mori could see. High and higher still. Past the setting sun and the rising moon. To a place where dragons play.